Emma Tom is a Sydney-based writer, broadcaster and musician. Her first novel, *Deadset*, won the 1998 Commonwealth Writers' Prize for Asia and the South Pacific. Her last book was *Something about Mary: from girl about town to Crown Princess*. This is her fifth book.

Other published titles in the NOW Australia series

Bali: Paradise Lost?

Emma Tom

PLUTO PRESS AUSTRALIA

First published in 2006 by
Pluto Press Australia
PO Box 617
North Melbourne Victoria 3051
www.plutoaustralia.com

Commissioning Editor Tony Moore
Editor Nadine Davidoff
Cover design by Peter Long
Typeset by Midland Typesetters
Printed and bound by Hyde Park Press

Australian Cataloguing in Publication Data

Tom, Emma.
    Bali : Paradise Lost?
    ISBN 1 86403 353 3.
    ISBN 978 186403 353 3
    1. Australians – Travel – Indonesia – Bali Island. 2.
    Vacations – Indonesia – Bali Island. I. West, Andrew. II.
    Title. (Series : Now Australia ; 1).

910.892405986

Cover photograph courtesy of Getty Images.
Indonesia, Bali, Gianyar, Oleg dancer waits to perform,
sitting next to temple guardian.
© Martin Westlake

For all four S's

CONTENTS

I've Been to Bali Too

Sex and scandalous circumstance meant your first overseas trip was to Bali.

Which isn't to say that the postcard paradise favoured by Australia's working class was your first choice. Apart from that annoying Redgum song ('I've Been to Bali Too'), you didn't consider it dangerous enough. You'd spent most of your 21 years in a small country town and craved hazardous foreign adventure. Crippling jetlag. First contact with at least one cannibalistic indigenous civilisation with menstruation huts (which, thanks to a maverick feminist anthropologist, you now believed were a handy excuse for a girls' night in rather than oppressive tools of nose-bone patriarchies).

Instead, sex and scandalous circumstance led you to backpacker Bali.

The year was 1990. 'Love Shack' by the B-52's was on top of the charts and industrial-sized shoulderpads were finally claiming their rightful place in dank secondhand-store discount bins. Hawke, the messiah, still sat upon his

1

summit but sound neighbourly relations required more than lairy APEC shirts and games of golf. An upstart treasurer enamoured of the ageing Indonesian president was about to execute a coup and drag Australia kicking and screaming into Asia.

During this first trip to Bali, your outrageous personal arrangements as a partly-paid-for scarlet woman presented peril enough but you did your best to up the danger ante by gobbling insect-infested street grub and allowing a grinning, knife-wielding stranger to lead you deep into the jungle. Tragically enough, the only physical harm you sustained was the result of surrendering to a shameful craving for Western food. Even 'I've Been to Bali Too' did not prepare you for the long night you spent heaving semi-digested spaghetti carbonara into the bathtub of a dirt-cheap Ubud *losmen*.

Four years later, you returned on a five-star journalistic junket. It was 1994. An Indonesian firing squad executed three foreigners for heroin trafficking as President Suharto – the autocrat who ran his country as a personal franchise – prepared to host APEC's signing of the Bogor Declaration on free trade. Wonderbras, heroin chic and the phrase 'the new black' were all new blacks.

Wined and dined by Bali's tourism tsars, you wandered lost and drunk through luxury resorts sprawling across hectares of manicured lawns and fountains. You didn't drink arak palm wine with the locals or use secret Balinese slang to disarm overenthusiastic sarong-sellers. You cruised some harbour or another on a zillion-dollar yacht and watched with deep melancholy as a daisy chain of tourists riding an inflatable banana mowed down a crab drifting out to sea on a hot-pink rubber thong.

Respectably careered and recently partnered, this

second trip was the perfect opportunity to 'do Bali' without the malignant guilt of another messy personal snarl. But you were careless and nihilistic and betrayed your lover back home with a haughty Czech heiress whose bikini glittered and whose hotel bed was the size of a swimming pool.

In 1998 you returned again, this time on honeymoon after a lightning, rock star marriage. You were too smitten to realise that Australia's relationship with its enormous neighbour was on the rocks. That President Suharto had resigned and *reformasi* was rising. That Australia's intervention in East Timor would leave sovereignty-obsessed Indonesians hateful and bitter for years. You were living the honeymoon cliché. And you and your dishevelled new husband were not alone. Shortly after jets of water inexplicably begun spouting from the ceiling on the plane commute to Denpasar, the pilot concluded his 'Hello, You Are Now in a Plane' speech by welcoming honeymooners Mr and Mrs X and congratulating them on their recent nuptials. The rioting was instantaneous.

'My apologies,' the pilot said over the loudspeaker while two flight attendants gazed at the water raining down on cattle-class with 'Why are we here?' or perhaps 'Why are *you* here?' expressions on their deeply painted faces. 'I'm terribly sorry, but it has just been brought to my attention that we have thirty or forty honeymooning couples on board today,' he continued, sounding rather ill. 'So congratulations and good luck to all of you.' The mess of newlyweds gazed into each other's eyes before returning to the in-flight reading material which revealed that Steven Spielberg had won an Oscar for *Saving Private Ryan* and that *Entertainment Weekly* regarded big-bosomed archaeologist Lara Croft as an 'it girl'.

Despite the pilot's blessings and your high decibel love, the rock star marriage did not last and the divorce papers were filed in August 2003 – the same month you'd planned a fourth visit to Bali with your mother and brother. This trip was to heal a family fight from the previous Christmas, an argument that started over the use of a family computer mouse but soon morphed into a vile beast with tentacles stretching into unspeakable crevices of the past. Your mother and brother had only recently resumed talking to you after months of estrangement. The Bali trip was a big deal.

Then terrorists blew up the JW Marriott Hotel in Jakarta and the destination you once dismissed as not dangerous enough became too terrifying a prospect. You marvelled at the travel wimp you'd become as you made the heartbreaking decision to cancel – losing $1366 on flights and accommodation – and waved off your mother and brother at the airport when they decided to carry on without you. When she returned, your mother framed the photo of your beaming brother risking rabies in the Sacred Monkey Forest and hung it up in the loungeroom. Seeing it would always make you sniffle.

After that trip that wasn't, you couldn't get Bali out of your head. You pored over your photographs from that first visit, barely recognising the blonde backpacker with the kamikaze personal life. Bali had also changed. Your big, white nation used to consider that ancient island its own but bombs were replacing the Bintang beer. When Paddy's Bar and the Sari Club went up in 2002, the hospitals flooded with bodily fluids and volunteers used curtains for bandages. When Raja Restaurant and Jimbaran Bay were detonated in 2005, the decapitated heads of suspected suicide bombers were beamed across the world. After the blast, local cops collected strips of bomber flesh in buckets. 'Look,' one cameraman observed, 'bomber penis.'

Australia gagged. This wasn't the comfortable cliché Redgum sang about in the 1980s. This was some incomprehensible new front of a war supposed to be confined to deserts on the other side of the planet. This was betrayal.

Indonesia added insult to injury in 2004 when a pretty Gold Coast shop girl was arrested at Denpasar Airport with a stash of pot she swore wasn't hers. Australian shockjocks called the judges apes and demanded their tsunami money back as John Howard and Indonesia's President Susilo Bambang Yudhoyono struggled to keep hold of the diplomatic steering wheel. The waters were muddied when nine more Australians were apprehended at the airport with a fortune in heroin strapped to their young bodies, but the nation's shock and outrage continued. Few knew or cared that Bali's reputation as a paradise was the self-serving and simplistic creation of Dutch colonialists; that its history was full of slave-trading, opium-smoking and widow-burning. The dominant view was that these changes were terrible and new. Bali was not supposed to be about severed heads, impenetrable legal systems and firing squads. Ordinary Australians were supposed to be able to holiday there like kings. The restaurants were not supposed to explode.

Like the blonde backpacker version of yourself at 21, the island of the gods had become unrecognisable. So, in March 2006, sixteen years after your first visit, you decided to return to try to make sense of a place and a past that suddenly seemed foreign.

TWO

I Love Room

Indonesia's draconian drug laws may not be much help to Bali's hoteliers but they're drumming up great business for God. We all know how it goes: Australian kiddie goes to Kuta and gets busted with drugs at the airport. Australian kiddie faces life behind Balinese bars. Australian kiddie finds God (or, in the case of pill-packing bikini models, Muhammad).

Cynics call it the road to Denpasar.

You – turncoat that you are – have experienced a similar conversion vis-à-vis Schapelle Corby. During the great boogie-board bag debate, you were a non-believer in her hysterical protestations of innocence. 'Well, look at the facts,' you railed over watercoolers and dinner parties. 'She arrived in Bali with a bongtastic bagful of dope. She couldn't prove anyone else put it there and her defences bordered on Bart Simpson-esque.'

After deflecting the inevitable accusations of cynicism and lack of compassion, you took a breath and ranted on. 'The *prima facie* case would have had legs anywhere,' you blustered. 'And what were her only two defences? "Someone else must have done it" and "I'm not the drug-smuggling type." The former is used by almost everyone who pleads not guilty to a crime and is useless unless accompanied by some actual evidence. The latter is based on the erroneous premise that all drug dealers have greasy hair, shifty moustaches and spiderweb tattoos on their elbows.'

Now that you're the one on the road to Denpasar, you've been born again. You turn up at Sydney's international airport towing a new, hard-shell suitcase with two key locks, two combination locks and a bolted security strap, convinced mustachioed barons with elbow tatts are about to make you their mule. At check-in, you join a congregation of Corby converts. Everyone's baggage is in bondage. Even flimsy fabric sportsbags sag with locks and chains.

Your government's view on travelling to Bali is simply not to. The Smart Traveller website run by the Department of Foreign Affairs and Trade warns of kidnappings, avian influenza and explosions. 'We advise you to reconsider your need to travel to Indonesia, including Bali, at this time due to the very high threat of terrorist attack,' it reads. 'We continue to receive a stream of reporting indicating that terrorists are in the advanced stages of planning attacks against Western interests in Indonesia against a range of targets, including places frequented by foreigners.'

Here at the airport, however, everyone has a 'We'll be okay because' mantra to justify why the warning does not apply to them.

The Corby clones carrying shrink-wrapped backpacks that look like crushed salad rolls: 'We'll be okay because we're staying outside Kuta.'

The middle-aged couple who buy hermetically sealed sprout sandwiches and nod approvingly as their meals are mammogrammed between industrial-sized toasting irons in the waffle shop: 'We'll be okay because our friends in Bali said we'd be okay.'

The young couple still slurping at each other's necks as they are funnelled onto the plane: 'We'll be okay because lightning doesn't strike twice.' Informed that Bali has already been bombed twice, the lovers shrug and keep slurping: 'Oh, in that case we'll definitely be okay. Lightning never strikes three times.'

You search for a mantra and fail. Working in the media makes it way too easy to fantasise about future horror headlines. You wonder what photo the papers will use when you come down with killer bird flu during a shock suicide smack raid and hope it won't be the one from your day-old passport. The new government rules ban teeth-showing in mug shots and your oddly pursed lips make you look like a terrorist barramundi. During the five-and-a-half-hour flight you fall asleep and dream of Schapelle's banana-sized marijuana buds and a bucket of fleshicated monkey head. In your dream, the word 'fleshicated' makes perfect sense.

Ngurah Rai Airport is just as you remember it. There are cement pylons wearing gold skirts, uniformed security dudes and a thick, fragrant heat. What's new is the anxious chatter about how to avoid being Corbied. 'When they come up to the carousel and ask, "Is this bag yours?" don't say anything,' one woman waiting at the wooden immigration desks tells another. 'Don't touch it until you've checked to see if anyone's tampered with the locks.' Another says locks are useless, that corrupt airport security staff have skeleton keys that open everything.

Two gamelan players pound out a manic tune beneath a television flashing images of rural life and gun-polishing. Next to them is a big black and orange sign saying the penalty for bringing drug (singular) into Bali is death. You can't imagine what it would be like to read this knowing you have marijuana bananas in your surf sack or a stash of smack gaffed to your groin.

When you collect your fortressed luggage and make it through customs unarrested, it is almost anticlimactic. You walk out of the airport feeling shallow, wondering how much you've really changed since that first time you arrived as scandal girl.

—

Despite what they said in the tearoom, the affair wasn't something you'd planned. You were eighteen. You didn't plan what you were going to do between one cigarette and the next. It was the late 80s and you'd just started work as a cadet journalist on the small country newspaper in your small country town. At school, youth workers told your year to prepare itself for unemployment. When the newspaper editor rang to say you'd passed the interview, you couldn't believe you'd been hired as the only thing you'd ever wanted to be; apart from a *Countdown* dancer or an orthodontist. Every day you arrived at the office convinced it would be your last.

The newspaper had a cadet counsellor, a senior writer with a leather jacket and a South African accent. The cadet counsellor was smart and droll and one of those pillars that keeps communities standing. He ripped your work to shreds and you hung off every word, awe-struck. When the two of you started sleeping together, it was as if his wife and three daughters lived on another planet.

You remember as if it were yesterday the night he arrived red-eyed on your doorstep with a small, beaten suitcase. Seventeen years your senior, and the cadet counsellor looked as though he could barely stand. At work, your colleagues called you a homewrecker and accused you of trying to fuck your way to the top. They said the cadet counsellor was ghost-writing all your stories. Maybe they called him names too, but you doubted it. The thesaurus contains hardly any entries for fallen men.

The cadet counsellor moved into a vinyl bachelor flat above a disco in town. You tried socialising as a legitimate couple but it was always hard. You were heavy with guilt and responsibility and the conviction that everyone knew, and that soon you would pay. You sent off job applications to every newspaper in Sydney.

In 1990, the two of you went to an election night party at the big beach house of Helen Caldicott, the peacenik physician running for the federal seat of Richmond. The mother of your best friend's ex-boyfriend didn't win, but the shower of preference confetti in her wake meant the federal leader of the National Party was ousted by Neville Newell, a Labor candidate so low-key he'd been nick-named Neville Who? The cadet counsellor wrote an article about these things for the newspaper and won $2690 in Qantas vouchers at a big journalistic awards night in Newcastle.

That's when he offered to buy you a plane ticket.

Bali wasn't your first choice. Asia had just replaced Europe as Australia's favoured holiday destination (in 1981, 378,000 Australians visited compared with 210,000 three years earlier) and you couldn't see the point of travelling to a foreign country overflowing with boozed- and sexed-up ockers. But $2690 didn't buy much in the way of airfares back in 1990 and you were desperate for a departure gate. Just that week you'd run into a sporting hero from school who also hadn't left town yet. Thanks to the attentions of his mother, he was yet to make a bed. It was horrific.

So, like so many of your compatriots, cost and convenience won out and you planned your first overseas experience as a budget traveller in Bali.

Determined not to become a Kuta cliché, you read everything you could lay your hands on. Fascinated by Bali's animistic reinvention of the Hinduism imported by ancient Indian traders, you hypocritically dismissed all Western influences as corrupting. Pressed to date the demise of the real Bali, you would have nominated 1597, the year the Dutch sea captain Cornelius de Houtman 'discovered' the island. As far as you were concerned, all cultural change occurring before that date was pure and all cultural change that followed was tainted. So what if a barbaric slave-trade had been roaring along in Bali since the 10th century? Historical dynamism and 'glocalisation' (an academic term describing the way local forces interpret and use global ones) would not enter your frame of reference for another decade-and-a-half.

Despite trying hard to resist the imperialist Western running dog tendency to exoticise the 'other', you were secretly captivated by the extremes of Balinese history – such as the revelation that de Houtman had spent time with a king who had two hundred wives, a chariot pulled by white buffalo and a phalanx of dwarves with bodies bent to resemble traditional daggers. Also awfully un-PC was your transfixion with the ancient Balinese practice of *suttee* and human sacrifice at cremations. One old painting showed a stunning widow smiling enigmatically as she slid an enormous dagger through her right shoulder and out her left breast. Embarrassingly enough, you found this erotic stoicism irresistibly sexy. Flummoxed about whether women's rights should trump indigenous practice (let alone politically incorrect arousal), you lit another cancer-rific Indonesian clove cigarette and decided to think about it later.

According to your books, tourism in Bali was invented by the Dutch in the early 20th century. In *Bali: A Paradise Created*, Adrian Vickers wrote that this was partly due to guilt over colonial massacres and partly because of a paternalistic desire to protect the 'traditional', to package Bali as a living museum. The 1920s was also when the paradise tag began being tossed around. It was an odd choice given the bloodiness of Bali's past. Apart from the human sacrifice thing, there'd been numerous nasty deaths from famines, poxes and volcanic eruptions. Not to mention the bloody local battles, the bloody colonial wars and the bloody slaughter of 100,000 Balinese communists in the 60s. (Weirdly enough, this relatively recent massacre left little trace in the Australian consciousness.) Locals were also infamous for their suicidal commitment to *puputan*, the practice of dying honorably in battle rather than surrendering. During one campaign in Denpasar, women with spears were said to have advanced towards armed Dutch troops, calmly and resolutely seeking death while carrying their children.

Not surprisingly, the colonising Dutch billed the locals as unpredictable savages in urgent need of civilisation. Much was made of the island's magical rituals and exorcisms, of its rigid caste system and the heavy use of opium in its royal courts. The peasants were written off as lazy thugs and the royals as debauched despots. During one treaty negotiation with the Dutch, a king was said to have demanded (and to have received) a live rhinoceros for his rituals. Another boasted eight hundred wives. In the 1920s, however, the Dutch gave Bali and its occupants an Island of Eden makeover.

The first thrill-seekers to arrive in paradise were rich Americans and Europeans drawn by promises of titillating witches, prepubescent dancing girls and bevies of bare-breasted beauties. Debate about whether Bali could survive international tourism began immediately and became a wildly successful selling point. Come quickly, the tourists were told, come see this fragile island before crass rubber-neckers like you destroy it forever. This was one of the great advantages of manufacturing paradise: you could always promote it as being in perilous danger of being lost. Famous early arrivals included Barbara Hutton, Georges Clemenceau, H.G. Wells, Charlie Chaplain, Noel Coward and Margaret Mead, many of whom gathered in the Ubud home of the flamboyant gay painter, Walter Spies, and his pet monkey.

Tourism crashed during World War II but became an integral part of nation-building after Indonesia declared independence in 1945. As luck would have it, this was also around the time the bare boobs of Bali were finally obscured. After unsuccessful modesty drives by the Dutch (as well as by members of the Balinese nationalist movement in the 1930s), the Sukarno-endorsed governor of Bali finally succeeded in the early 60s to clothe the top halves of Balinese women.

By then, Australian cinema-goers had received a bawdy introduction to their island neighbour via the slapstick 1952 Bing Crosby and Bob Hope musical comedy, *Road to Bali*. This bizarre creation is worth seeing for the introductory monologue alone. 'The Commonwealth of Australia,' drones an unseen narrator, 'land of many frontiers. Lone stepping stone across the vast Pacific to the mysterious, brooding islands of the Malaysian archipelago. Last outpost of the art and culture of the Western world ... '

Road to Bali begins in Melbourne where Crosby and Hope take jobs as deep-sea treasure-divers to escape the clutches of a couple of women to whom they'd made the mistake of proposing. The next hour-and-a-half is a bizarre mishmash of tropical island clichés as the outlandishly racist song-and-dance men battle cannibals, head-hunters, talking volcanoes, randy gorillas, singing sheep, giant squid, chopsticks and shrunken women coaxed out of cobra baskets by 'fun flutes'.

In the 1970s, Australia's magic mushroom-loving surfers began arriving at brooding Bali's brand-new Ngurah Rai Airport in search of very different sorts of treasures. Jakarta was unimpressed. According to Adrian Vickers:

> The bulk of the tourists were not the expected rich Americans that an emerging nation craved to boost its revenues, but the new breed of Western middle-class youth, hippies. Bali was at the bottom end of the 'Asian highway' which stretched from London and Amster-dam to Sydney, with every spot on the way a paradise of free love and cheap drugs.

According to Australian scholars Richard White and Ingrid Bown, Australia's shift from the British umbilical cord to an engagement with Asia and the Pacific was largely due to its holidaymakers. They say early Asian excursions were carried out with humility and a firm belief in their value as learning experiences. It was only towards the end of the 20th century that cheap airfares enabled antipodeans to holiday in Bali in pursuit of hedonism alone. Jet-setters in certain states discovered they could nip over in slightly less time than it took to cross the Sydney Harbour Bridge in peak-hour traffic, and that accommodation was available for only slightly more than the bridge's toll. Bali became the first overseas travel destination for ordinary Aussies who wanted a break from candida-ridden caravan parks but who couldn't afford Europe. For many years it was one of the few foreign countries where the dollar's exchange rate wasn't the punchline to an aggravating joke. In Bali, Australians were literally and financially huge. They towered in enormous, fleshy hulks over a lithe local populace that seemed to forgive them everything.

Two weeks before you too left to become a rupiah millionaire, you turned 21 and got drunk on sickly sweet Spumante at a heavily ballooned birthday party in a country hall. Two of the cadet counsellor's grown-up friends gave you a gold locket containing his portrait as a peace offering. It should have made you feel better but it didn't. You put a photograph of the beloved family rottweiler – now dead – in the locket's spare window but the sight of your lover's face still made you unspeakably sad.

You and the cadet counsellor bounced around in rough air above the Indian Ocean. You wrote about the sky in your journal and made manic calculations about your tight daily budget. He amused you with accents and watched a Steve Martin movie. After a three-hour sunset, the plane circled over the sandy cliffs and fires of Bali waiting for permission to land. By the time you disembarked, it was night. You thought the wall of heat on the tarmac came from the plane's exhaust but you were wrong. This was what you'd been waiting for: crushing, foreign heat.

At immigration, four long lines looped back from desks patrolled by guards in khaki uniforms with macraméd armbands. If there was a drug sign, you didn't notice it.

Overwhelmed by the cloud of business cards and screamed offers of transport outside the airport, you coveted the circumstances of two businessmen collected by a sharply dressed meeter-and-greeter holding a 'Mr Daniels' sign. After a bewildered attempt at bartering, you and the cadet counsellor paid a short, acned man to take you to a *losmen* (the lowest of Bali's low-end hotels) you'd picked out of the guidebook on the plane. 'Nice car, nice car,' the acne man kept saying as he ploughed through a bunch of roadworkers who yelled at the cab through the gloom. You tried to look cool but unlit streets snaked crazily in every direction. You couldn't believe how alien, how precarious, how wild everything was. It was nothing like the manicured, all-Australian theme park you'd expected.

The first *losmen* was full and the driver said he'd take you to his brother-in-law's. He parked the cab, snatched one of your bags and disappeared down hell lane. It was pitch black and you remembered one of the guidebooks warning that a certain percentage of Australian tourists return from Bali in boxes. But you soon found a mantra and told yourself you'd be okay because that bit of the book was only directed at surfers blasé about rips and reefs.

Nice Car Nice Car's brother-in-law struck a hard bargain and demanded double what you'd hoped to spend. You gave him $17 and he gave you a coral tag with a number five on one side and the words *I Love Room* on the other. The cement cube was dark and stinking hot. The long, plastic shower nozzle was raping the stained toilet and everything smelled of piss. You took off your travelling clothes and fought with the dodgy plastic shower nozzle, wincing as diseased water streamed down your face. Later, you lay naked in the bed, listening to barking dogs and Indonesian pop songs through the mosquito-coiled darkness. You couldn't believe this was the place they called paradise.

At 5 a.m. some noxious cross between a dog and a rooster crowed outside the curtained hole in the wall that passed as a window. In the daylight, I Love Room looked even worse. The paint was peeling and the sheets were sticky. Outside, however, the grounds were stunning. There were thatched rooves, ferns in pots, fake gold paint and plants sprouting from everything. Across the path, a guy mopped a slate verandah by pushing a damp, brown T-shirt round with a stick. His shirt read, *If You're Rich I'm Single*. Women in rubber thongs placed offerings of fruit and flowers beside a lane filled with people cycling, walking and carrying. You wished you were the first person to arrive and not the brazilianth.

The man with the mop brought breakfast: fluorescent pawpaw with lime, white toast with the crusts cut off, and globulus yellow jam. The coffee was thick and milk-less and left a dark sludge at the bottom of your cup. After breakfast, you set off in search of the sea.

Only 8.30 in the morning and already everyone was yelling. *Youwanttransport? Youwannaseemyshop? Yousureyoudon'twanttransport?* You said no to an elephant and were offered a bong (no doubt some sort of Kuta code). Women in blue pyramid hats with white numbers squeezed your shoulders. *Youwantmassage?* Felt your hair.

Youwantplaits? Grabbed your hands. *Ahyouwantnails!* Guys opened boxes of watches into your face, so close the numbers blurred. A little kid selling leather bands blocked your path. You said no you said no you said no. 'I'll kill you,' he muttered under his breath. He only reached your waist. At the beach, the surf was flat and dirty, and you and the cadet counsellor took it in turns to swim and mind the wad of travellers' cheques.

Back at I Love Room, you said goodbye to a woman with a baby who'd been trained to kiss hands on command. The woman saw your ring, asked if it was gold and tried to pull it off. She looked offended when it stayed put. 'You married?' she asked. '*Belum*,' you replied. Not yet. It was the answer recommended by the guidebook which said a 'no' to this question was inconceivable. Social protocol demanded either a 'yes' or a 'real soon'.

You decided to catch a bus to Candidasa, a small fishing village on the east coast, and grimly rebuckled your back- packs. Yours was a massive suitcase that transformed into a wearable square via a trick zipper. The concept was terribly flash in theory but in practice left deep shoulder welts. After wandering through the heat for an hour, the straps felt as though they were rubbing against bare bone. Time and again you asked for directions to Bemo Corner (the main bus stop) and time and again you wandered in circles through a jungle of sarong stands and wind chimes. Eventually you gave up on the public transport and hailed a cab.

Candidasa was only a couple of centimetres away on the map but the trip took all day. The streets were apocalyptic and you sat in traffic-jams for hours. There was no right side of the road and the driver honked before all the bridges. He was Mr Easy Going until he ran down a cat and flipped. Maybe he said something about a totem. Maybe you just imagined it as you inched past all those crumbling cement houses and makeshift markets, all the while microwaving alive in the car. For lunch you ate with the cat-killer at a roadside stall where the chef stirred the wok with the same small broom she used to sweep the floor. You asked for extra chilli and ate everything.

Candidasa was nothing like the postcards. The tourist guff made it out to be the archetypal sand, surf and sea resort. But when you arrived, there was no sand left at all. Just giant cement sea walls to keep the water eating any more of the resorts. Apparently the problem was the harvesting of off-shore coral – coral used to make cement lime for hotels and I Love Room knickknacks.

Amazingly enough, your micro budget stretched to a bungalow that would have been beachside if there'd been any beach. The landlady lay on a wooden platform outside her office drinking rice wine. She was loud and jabby but her bungalows were stunning. There were a dozen or so scattered across a thick lawn full of coconut palms and fawn cows with big eyes and bells. You read Jane Austen beside the sea, watched the sunset sizzle and told yourself that this was the sort of place rich people went on honeymoon. For a moment you thought everything was finally going to be all right. Then, the next morning, your lover shyly, self-consciously suggested sex. And without even knowing what you were doing, you told him it was over.

THREE

I Cannot Be
Biannual

'That was easy,' you say when Wayan the van man collects you right outside customs at the airport.

There's an expensive new Blue Bird cab brand in Kuta running a fleet of candy-coloured mobile freezers, but you booked a no-name minivan from Australia.

'It's always easy when there's only one guest to find,' Wayan replies. 'No one comes to Bali any more. It's a good time for silence. We're all bankrupt!' The hilarity of this last comment leaves him slapping his thighs and wiping his eyes.

(Australians always talk about the beauty of the Balinese people. Less frequently mentioned is their black sense of humour, though one guidebook does warn that local onlookers may howl with laughter if you fall over in the street and break your leg.)

As you help load your hog-tied mega case into the back of Wayan's van, you ask what happens to local people who go bankrupt in Bali. Once again, he can barely contain himself. 'They stay at home and cry!' he shrieks.

Australians are also staying at home. Figures from the Bureau of Statistics show that only 16,500 visited Indonesia in February 2006 – half what they were in the same month in 2005. Pundits reckon the young party girls and boys are now choosing booze cruises on ships they would once have written off as floating nursing homes.

Wayan stops and starts through the Denpasar back streets. The minibus's airconditioning is sluggish. It's like an esky – slightly cooler inside than out, but only just. You half-expect to find your feet stewing among bags of frozen ice and par-thawed sausages. Shouting paperboys shove foreign newspapers against the windows, sprinting alongside as the lights change. If you don't respond to broken English, they try again in broken Japanese, in broken German, in broken Dutch until it all melds together into a wild stream of Frankenspruik. The streetscape is still a mess of crumbling houses and shops but now there are also American fastfood chains – glistening cathedrals where pilgrims come to worship the almighty burger, doughnut and fried chicken drumstick. Bali's infestation of wart-hoggy dogs is as bad as it ever was, but now the mutts must navigate MYOB training centres, multi-storied bridal studios and towering billboards advertising huge men with electronic equipment. You ask Wayan what these billboards are really advertising but even he can't say for sure.

The road to Candidasa is smoother than it used to be, but when it isn't, it's catastrophic. Killer potholes and puddles of wet cement are fenced off with haphazard arrangements of witches' hats and driftwood. There are canals solid with garbage and deep drains brimming with bike tyres. One gaping chasm in the highway is marked by a dead tree someone has jammed in upright, a barren floral arrangement in a bitumen vase. Hours pass and you don't see a single white face. Back in 1990, this strangeness was all you wanted. Now it's eerie.

Outside of Denpasar, Bali looks more as you remember it. There's a baby in formal dress propped up the front of a speeding motorcycle, fat neck concertinaed beneath the weight of an oversized helmet. There's a 'buffet festival', something called Splash Bakery and a sign for a shop offering antiques made to order. Wayan drives you through a stunning mountain village where naked men soap their genitals in a river beside the road. The guidebooks tell you not to look when people wash like this, that such bathers wear a cloak of invisibility, but it's hard not to stare. Next to the see-through men is a car with a bamboo cage of poultry strapped to the roof. Next to that is a minivan with a slogan that reads: *Electricity For a Better Life*.

On the outskirts of Candidasa, Wayan asks about your travel plans and offers his business card in case you want to book his esky again. The card was originally for a Jimbaran Bay seafood restaurant specialising in squid, *barakuda* and *garupa*. 'Ignore that,' Wayan says. 'My restaurant is closed now. No one goes to Jimbaran any more.' His is the first of seven business cards you receive with the details of a beachside seafood restaurant scribbled out and replaced with a number for a cab.

You can't remember the name of the break-up bungalows from your first trip so you check into another place at the foot of Candidasa's mountain. Your room is wooden and has a verandah overlooking a lily pond. There are dueling dragonflies, goldfish the size of reef sharks and a bristling room temple dressed in an orange and white skirt with a red and gold front pouch. Struggling to remember the combinations to all your suitcase locks, you sheepishly plug in your excess of technology: your laptop, your portable speakers, your mobile phone, your keyboard, your mouse. There are written warnings about the room temple (don't desecrate it with wet washing) and the mosquitoes (*It is a good idea to wear mosquito repellent if you are particularly attractive to mosquitoes*). No explanation is offered for the squad of muscular lizards performing military manoeuvres up and down the walls.

For dinner, you eat stirfry with extra chilli in the hotel restaurant. The noodles are the consistency of tape worms but taste amazing. You've forgotten your glasses and struggle to read the drinks blackboard behind the bar. The shooter theme turns out to be testicular. There are Slippery Nuts and Melon Balls which you forgo for a ginger martini and a latte that comes with a towering head of milk froth, cinnamon and ants. Tinkling traditional tunes pipe from the restaurant stereo but these are drowned out by the rockers at the Iguana Café across the road. There are no punters in this cavernous venue but the band plays on regardless, belting out heavily accented versions of 'Sweet Home Alabama' by Lynyrd Skynyrd and 'What's Up?' by 4 Non Blondes.

You're the only diner in the restaurant and ask the waitress about business. She says there are definitely three other people staying at the hotel but you don't see any sign of them – not in the noisy restaurant, not in the curvy pool and not in the gift shop which says everything is unexpectedly half price. The waitress asks how long you're staying and sighs when you tell her it's only a night, that tomorrow you'll leave her with only her three invisible guests for company.

After the noodles, you walk into the chaos of the main drag and find a concrete shop selling pirate DVDs. You ask the woman behind the counter if her discs play on

Australian DVD players and she says they should, her boss is from Perth. You buy *Brokeback Mountain* for $2 and walk on. There are no streetlights and the road is full of potholes and screaming traffic. A young man suggests you climb onto the back of his scooter for a ride and you want to tell him to stop wasting his time; that you've suddenly become so old, shooter menus are blurry even before you start drinking. Eventually you reach a strange strip of ocean on the edge of town and realise you are lost. You give the name of your hotel to a couple at a roadside stall but they say sorry, there is no such place. A vast steel sign advertising a beer garden collapses into the road and every-one falls about in the dark guffawing – even the three motorcyclists who are nearly sliced and diced. A snarling dog bails you up against a wall and a watching sarong-seller decides this is fantastically funny, too.

'Don't worry,' he smirks, pointing at the dog (which is now producing actual mouth foam), 'he's saying "Welcome to Bali".'

You retrace your steps and find your way back to the pirate DVD store. The boss from Perth emerges fat and sweaty from a nearby café or jungle compound. 'Didn't *Brokeback* work?' he asks by way of introduction. Clearly his employees keep him in the loop. The DVD pirate's eyes bulge through magnified glasses and his front tooth has snapped to a vampirish point. There's definitely something of the Marlon Brandos about this guy. Something about the way he slinks from the shadows, crazed, maybe, from too many years beyond the Do Lung Bridge. Instead of the horror, however, all this Marlon wants to talk about is the second season of the HBO television series *Deadwood*. He just loves it, just can't get enough of the all-swearing, all-whoring saloon owner, Al Swearengen.

You choose some more DVDs and the *Apocalypse Now* guy insists on putting them into his DVD player and playing the endings to show how well they work. Many don't, but he says the problem is his stuffed DVD player not his discs. Marlon can't boast enough about the quality of his illegal merchandise. 'They're second and third generation,' he says, as if you have the faintest idea what he's talking about. 'Nothing like that crap they sell in Kuta.' Of particular pride to him is the FBI copyright warning at the start. Later you realise this proves they weren't videoed over people's heads in cinemas the way they used to be. You walk into the night with Marlon calling *King Kong* after you. He can't believe you don't want to buy it.

When you finally find your way back to your hotel, you juggle another ginger martini up to your room and watch *Brokeback Mountain* on your laptop, which overheats as you balance it on your knees in bed. The DVD's volume is almost too low to hear the dialogue and every so often a warning flashes up saying the disc is for award consideration only. You switch on the subtitles.

In the original movie, Jack Twist makes an impassioned plea to his cowboy lover Ennis del Mar during one of their trysts on Brokeback Mountain:

You count the damn few times that we have been together in nearly twenty years and you measure the short fucking leash you keep me on and then you ask me about Mexico and you tell me you kill me for needing something that I don't hardly never get. You have no idea how bad it gets. I'm not you. I can't make it on a couple of high altitude fucks once or twice a year.

In the pirate version, the subtitles for this lengthy monologue are reduced to a pithy 39 words. 'You count several times we with time, last is you ask I,' they read (if read is not too optimistic a verb). 'And you inform I to kill, for something that I have never done. You is nothing; there is no ugly idea how that. I cannot be, biannual.'

You wonder whether these idiosyncratic deviations from E. Annie Proulx's original text have anything to do with Indonesia's growing Islamic backlash against the depravities of Western culture. A proposed anti-pornography law outlaws tight clothes and public dancing to pop music, imposing daunting jail terms on husbands and wives who kiss in public as well as on anyone flaunting a 'sensual body part' such as their navel. It's bad news for Australian sheilas sunbaking on Kuta beaches as well as gay cowboys in American DVDs.

You fall asleep as unsensually as possible as thunderclaps and late-night roosters crow between the tireless sets of the Iguana Café covers band.

The next morning you order muesli in the deserted hotel restaurant and are delivered a milk-less mix of roasted peanuts, cashews and sultanas. Your opinion of these eccentric Balinese takes on Western staples has changed. You used to think they were like bats, neither beast nor bird (a metaphor, incidentally, that Chinese scholar Tang Guanghui once used to describe Australia's flittings between East and West). Now, however, you see such hybridisations as having a legitimate genre all of their own. It's not just the food, either. There's also something decidedly battish about those *Brokeback Mountain* subtitles. 'I cannot be biannual,' is neither English nor Indonesian, yet its resonance is undeniable. It reeks of intensity and integrity, of a high-voltage personality for whom there are only ever two courses of action: all or nothing.

After another ant latte, you walk out in search of your past. Navigating the shattered footpath, you try to remember the exact reasons you broke up with the cadet counsellor, but the memories are slippery. Your extensive diary notes from that first trip make no mention of the break-up, or even that you travelled with a companion at all. You know that many of your media colleagues would applaud this expunging of the personal on the grounds that 'real' journalism is untainted by the subjectivity or ego of the author. But now, trying to make sense of why things happened the way they did, you wish your old journals were not such a first-person-free zone.

As always, your thoughts are interrupted by the constant streetside yodelling. *Youwantsnorklingdarling? Youamerican? Maybeyoucomejoinusjusttalkingorsomethingpleasebaby?*

Candidasa looks just like the wild jungle village you remember. The only difference is that this time, you're one of the only outsiders. As you pick your way around a green seaside lake, a little girl exits from a hole in a stone wall carrying a load of dirty dishes that she dips carefully into the scum. There's a battered sign pointing to 'the marketplace of leisure' and a boy selling photocopies of a week-old Australian newspaper. Further down the road is a shop sign reading *Economic Laundry and Play Station*, a restaurant offering *Spaggety Carbonary* and *Crazy Pancake*, a scooter carrying two small women and three huge children. The mascot of the Candidasa Fitness Club is a frog lifting a dumbbell. You catch a glimpse of yourself in a shop window and grimace. You'd smeared yourself with a thick layer of sunscreen gel and insecticide, and have started to flake.

There's no sign of the break-up bungalows and, after a while, the road writhes off into a thick jungle of hens and cattle and fires and filth and pissing men. A man on a bike blocks your path, asking if you'd like to see his shop. You say no and walk around him. He catches up and says no worries, you're getting pretty close to his other shop, now. You say you really don't want to buy anything and he offers transport. Nice massage. The inevitable snorkel. When you refuse all this, he stops to think, then gives you a sly look. 'How about I take you into the jungle for a while,' he says. 'It'll be, you know, something like a trek.' Alarmed, you turn too fast and twist your ankle in a gutter choked with plastic bags. And as you hobble back towards the main road – desperate to see just one of the hundreds of tourists who used to crawl though Candidasa – you think back to the first time a stranger offered to lead you into the Balinese jungle …

—

Once the initial shock of your unplanned split with the cadet counsellor had subsided, the two of you sat in the beautiful bungalow and talked logistics. You'd expected to have to spend the next three weeks travelling alone but he said that was stupid, that the two of you might as well try to stick together and make the best of things. So off you went. At Lovina Beach, three old women braided your hair. At Tanah Lot, Javanese tourists hauled you into their happy snaps. At a café at the volcanic lake you snorted at the menu's spelling errors, amazed that the two of you could spend so much time laughing. You never stayed anywhere for long. Ducks in rice paddies. Piglets on poles. Endless dogs eating endless religious offerings. Eventually all the moving around got too much and the two of you bought a wooden chess set and settled down in a $4 a night *losmen* in Ubud. Separate beds. So much chess.

On Christmas Eve, you paid $2 for tickets to a cremation. The cadet counsellor thought it tacky. 'Watch granny burn,' he'd mocked. But you thought of the beautiful dying widow with the breast dagger and insisted. A bus took you to a village and dumped you beside a road with hundreds of other ticket-holding Australian and American tourists. During the long wait you were bartered into submission by tight formations of saleswomen with cargo piled high on their heads. Flutes were blown in your faces. Chess sets were opened like porno briefcases. Porno briefcases were opened offering racks of film. After an hour-and-a-half, you'd been bullied into buying two sarongs, two cold drinks, three shirts, a bronze Buddha, a pointy hat, a wooden cat and a blue pants-and-top set that hadn't been hemmed. The cadet counsellor bought two sarongs, two cold drinks, a shirt, a painted coconut shell and a banana.

You took revenge by snickering at people's English. The locals struggled with f's and v's, calling you their *prend* and offering *beep sate* and *progs' legs* in the restaurants. Laughing probably made you a bad person but your concerted efforts to speak Indonesian and Balinese also left everyone in stitches.

When the cremation procession finally began, you followed the surging crowd into what you thought was a temple but which turned out to be the house of the grieving family. The dead man was a teacher. His framed black-and-white photograph sat on top of a swaying bamboo funeral pyre, incongruous among the flowers, tinsel and holy men. The coffin was a flimsy pine affair and teetered wildly as a team of important men tried to hoist it upwards. Material ripped, the sides of the box flapped and the dead teacher nearly cannonballed into the ooh-ing and ah-ing crowd.

When the recalcitrant casket was finally tethered, someone passed up two screaming chickens dangling by the legs. Then, after an age of nothing, the pyre-bearers suddenly leapt to their feet and sprinted down the hill – saturated by hooting youths aiming hoses. The towering funeral architecture had a life of its own and skidded sideways like a semi-trailer in an oil spill. At one point, half the dripping bearers collapsed to their knees, pockets bursting and raining coins. A few people cried but most just shouted and sky-larked. A tour guide explained this was because it could take years to save for a Balinese cremation. The grief was rarely fresh.

When the coffin-carriers reached the charred and hilly cremation ground, they wrestled their load onto a green banana trunk stage then retreated to smoke, lick their wounds and reclaim their thongs. Rituals were performed. Someone connected a makeshift flame-thrower to a drum of petrol in a tree and aimed a dragon's blast of fire directly at the body. The coffin burned away and soon the head and shoulders of the dead man emerged charred and dripping. Cremation attendants poked the burning wood while others scraped bits of body from under the fire and put them to one side. Half an hour passed and still the cadaver did not change shape. You marvelled at the resilience of human flesh and the fact that watching a corpse burning could actually get boring. You joined the rest of the tourists shuffling towards the revving minivans while the dead school teacher kept fighting the fire like a green potato in a barbecue. No women with daggers committed glamorous suicide.

In Ubud, the cadet counsellor beat you at chess and read to you from a book of literary fantasy. Every morning you walked through the Sacred Monkey Forest to watch rival kingdoms of grey macaques battle over chip packets and camera bags. Like everyone else, you ignored the signs saying *Don't Touch* and encouraged the thieving primates to squat on your head and shoulders for photos. The monkeys were unpredictable and moody. Mutilated and paw-less from fighting, they bared their teeth and pulled at their dicks. One morning they sunk their teeth deep into the shoulder of a sunburned American with a bulging money belt and crisping thighs.

On the other side of the monkey forest was a tiny shop where school children queued to buy ancient lemonade and sweaty plastic bags of sweets. The little stall was dusty and dirty and the woman behind the counter kept her prized bricks of cheese in cardboard boxes out the back. Next door was a camp of itinerant artists who sold ugly, dark woodcarvings of pigs fucking pigs, pigs fucking women, pigs fucking frogs, and angels with enormous cocks. This timber fuckfest was in stark contrast to the strict entry regulations at a nearby temple. *Attention*, read the black and white sign.

Those who are not allowed to enter the temple are ladies who are pregnant, ladies whose children have not got the first teeth, children whose first teeth not fallen out yet, ladies during their period, devotees getting impure due to death, mad ladies/gentlemen [and] those not properly dressed.

Past the mad ladies sign was a field of rice farmers who spent their breaks squatting by the road smoking. Every day you greeted them in tortured Indonesian and one day one of them followed to chat even though he couldn't believe you asked whether the dog sitting next to him had a name. 'What do you mean a name? It is a dog. Its name is dog.' Thanks to your books, you already knew that naming in Bali was a highly regulated affair. Given names were the same for both sexes and determined by birth order. The first child was called Wayan, Putu or Gede. The second was Made, Kadek or Nengah. The third was Nyoman or Komang, and the fourth was Ketut. If you had more than four children, you just started again from the beginning.

The rice man was a Made (pronounced Ma Day as in Make My). After putting you straight on the dog business, he said why not come to his village for lunch? 'It's just ten minutes that way,' he said, pointing into the jungle. You and the cadet counsellor looked at each other and shrugged. What did you have to lose?

Within minutes you'd dropped into a gorge and out of sight of the road. That's when you realised you didn't know anything about the rice man except, 'What is your name?' and 'Where are you from?'. You hadn't even asked, 'Are you married?' (thereby completing your Indonesian conversational triumvirate). You wondered about Made's rice knife with its curved blade catching the sun as he slashed grass from the path and turned to grin at your stumblings on the steep track. At least you'd got your woodcarving-buying frenzy out of the way the day before. Lugging two pigs fucking up that hill would have been beyond the pale.

Half an hour of hiking later and there was neither village nor lunch in sight. The sun was scorching and the knots in your stiff, new cremation sarong had started to chafe. You reached a river and the rice man sprang goat-like from boulder to boulder while you scratched and slipped. Now would be the perfect time, you thought. One foul sweep of his rice knife and it would all be over. All he'd have to do is slip it in through the shoulder and out through the breast.

The moment passed and you arrived at what you hoped was not a bridge: three bamboo poles propped loosely over a vertiginous drop. Made abandoned the goat-man act and edged sideways, eyeing the rapids with his rice knife held high for balance. You followed, shuffling forward over the shiny cylinders and wishing you also had a blade to brandish at your fear of falling. But mixed with the fear was the smug realisation that finally you were Off the Beaten Path, that just because you'd failed as a lover did not mean you couldn't succeed as a traveller.

A further half an hour later, the cadet counsellor spotted smoke and stone walls through the trees and the rice man stopped at a shabby bamboo hut that contained two restless fawn cows. They looked hungry for action and you kept expecting them to sway over and say, *You want nice cud chew? You want nice cow bell? You want nice walk over rice knife bridge of death? Special price for you.* Made led you through the silent streets of his village, past faces and pointing fingers appearing over doors and between walls. His house was like all the others: a dirty compound surrounded by gardens and stone walls. Three young sons production-lined paintings for tourists in a corner. A shrivelled old woman with reams of breasts offered the earth fruit, rice and flowers in palm-leaf baskets. Behind her was a line of ducks with mohawk top-knots and a crusty dog that ate everything she put down except the incense.

Made offered you seats on the tile verandah outside his room and left you and the cadet counsellor alone with a smashed television set and a fractured family photograph. A young woman appeared in a doorway with a baby. She smiled and lifted her shirt so her child could play with her nipples. Clearly some Balinese breasts had survived the purges. An eternity passed before the rice man reappeared with two cups of luke-warm black tea and a little white sack. You waved an invisible rice knife at your fear of contaminated water and stirred in three teaspoons of sugar and two large cockroaches. Made saw this and laughed. 'Drink up your tea,' he said. 'Drink it all up.' You fished out the cockroaches and watched them twitch soggily in your spoon.

Made disappeared again, returning much later with a plate of cold yellow and silver lumps on a plate. It was *pisang goreng*. Banana fritters. They were greasy but delicious so long as you didn't look down at the glistening grey slivers while you chewed. Again, your host left you to eat alone. When he finally returned with three brimming plates it was late in the afternoon. Made had apologised that lunch wouldn't be like it was in restaurants, but the food was amazingly good: rice, roasted nuts and an eye-wateringly hot clump of stringy meat that used to be one of the Sex Pistol ducks.

This time, Made dined with you, flicking bugs from his food as he chewed. Afterwards, you all leaned back in his bamboo chairs to chat. The conversation was interrupted by numerous dashes for your phrasebook which contained handy translations for 'I'm allergic to bees' and 'Good morning madam, I think my leg is broken' (just in case you wanted to crack an after-dinner joke). You were glad you saved *sudah kawin*? – are you married? – 'til now because it turned out to be a talking point. Made used to have a wife. That's how he got all the sons. But she left him and shacked up with another man from the village which was an ongoing source of shame. It was Made's sister who cooked. She lived on the other side of the village which was why it had taken so long. The rice man said he was looking for another woman to marry to look after his sons and their paintings. Any luck so far? 'Belum,' he said. Not yet.

You desperately wanted to ask more, like why he'd brought you here, like what was in it for him, like how many other first-time Australian tourists in Bali ended up drinking cockroaches and eating punk duck in a car-less village worlds from anywhere. But you'd run out of Indonesian and he'd exhausted his English, so the three of you just sat there smoking as the day got darker.

Many years later, as a travel writer, you spent three days on a city-sized oceanliner – one of the old-fashioned ones with velvet dining rooms and roast beef at every meal. 'The trip was okay,' you told your friends when you got home. 'But who'd have thought cruising would be so much like being on a boat?' When asked about that first visit to Indonesia, your reply was similar. 'The trip was okay,' you said. 'But who'd have thought Bali would be so much like being in a foreign country?' It was the third worldliness that got to you. The dirt, the pollution and the grinding poverty. No one you'd met earned more than $A45 a month. Promoting a place like this as paradise was the same expedient spin-job it had always been, but the Australian party crowd you'd seen and shunned in Kuta seemed to have bought the chimera. Cheap rooms, cheap beer and cheap bootleg cassettes of the B52's singing 'Love Shack'. All of it courtesy of cheap, cheap labour. Did any of those tanned Australian girls and boys ordering magic mushroom omelets in the cafés realise they were the new imperialists?

Two nights before you left Ubud, you and the cadet counsellor ate at a dodgy Italian restaurant and you got your first ghastly taste of Bali belly. You didn't touch spaghetti carbonara ever again after that night. Quite frankly, you thought you'd be the same about Bali.

———

Back in Candidasa in 2006, you re-emerge on the main drag and glance backwards at the badgerer on the bike, this new man who wants to lead you into the jungle. It's all over, you think. You'll never adventure like that again. And it's not just Bali with its travel warnings and terrorists. It's the whole world. The older you get, the more you just want to stay home.

You give up trying to find the break-up bungalows and head back to the hotel. That's when you see the door in the stone wall. You'd missed it the first time, distracted by all those screamed offers of snorkel. But as you step through the mouldy gap into a lightless courtyard, you realise it's the one. The drunken landlady is gone. Her wooden platform is now loaded with teenage girls and a boy watching a snowy TV. But the memories tsunami back and you ask if you can see a room.

One of the TV girls leads you along a track towards the hut where it all happened. The sunlight through the trees is muddy and there are no longer any cows but the sea is still as sparkly as ever. The TV girl opens the door and it takes a moment to make out the rotting fan lying unplugged beside the dingy double bed, the putrid pit of the shower, the walls caked with decades of human scum.

She asks for $20, expecting you to halve it, and you say maybe later. You can't believe this is it. The place you thought rich people stayed on honeymoon. In your memories it was an earthly heaven ruined by your hideousness. But now you realise it was most likely a dive, an absolute disaster all along.

You sit on a carved wooden bench looking out at the cement walls holding back the ocean and wish you could go back to comfort your cyclonic self from all those years ago, to tell the blonde with the stupid backpack that it'll be okay, that things really will get better. And as you head back to your hotel, you realise the other benefit of time travel is that you could warn version 21.1 of yourself not to give in and eat the spaghetti carbonara.

FOUR

Disco Riding Dusana

Nusa Dua has always patrolled its borders. Before the era of bomber heads in buckets, the decorative gates to this surreal enclave of swank resorts were supposed to keep out the riff-raff. Now the security guards are concerned with more deadly disturbances. 'Check bomb,' the driver cabbing you from Candidasa explains as the underside of his car is examined by armed guards holding mirrors on sticks. 'Also they are using metal protectors.'

This procedure happens again when you reach the gates of your hotel, though each time you pass through the security checks the routine is different. Sometimes the guards open the boot and 'protector' your luggage. Sometimes they just wink and nod at the driver. Other days they open the cab doors and stare long and hard before waving you through with tight lips and grim faces. It's hard to know what they're looking for during these intense eyeballings. After all, Indonesian Muslim extremists rarely have the handy Arabic accents and Osama beards so mesmerising to American airport staff.

Here, they look pretty much like everyone else.

Nusa Dua in southern Bali was established by Jakarta and the World Bank in the 1970s to insulate well-to-do tourists from the rest of the island. Manageable bites of Bali Lite in the form of traditional shows and dances were brought in at night when the international transients were feeling up to some culture. Not surprisingly, travel puritans have always derided Nusa Dua, with the Lonely Planet guidebook calling this wonderland of wall-to-wall luxury resorts a gilded ghetto. 'There are no independent developments, no hawkers, no *warung*, no traffic, no pollution and no noise,' it sniffs. 'You could be at any international tropical beach resort the world over.'

While Nusa Dua is home to a disproportionate number of stiff, white tablecloths and stiff, white guests, local idiosyncrasies do abound. The Nusa Dua design committee, for instance, rules that resorts be no higher than the coconut trees and that their layouts be modelled on Balinese architecture. Accordingly, buildings are structured into three parts: the world of the gods, the world of humans and the world of demons. Also represented architecturally is the human body, with traditional family compounds consisting of a head (the domestic temple), the arms (the bedrooms and living areas), the legs and feet (the kitchen and rice-storage building) and the rectum (the garbage dump). As the *Periplus Guide to Bali* gleefully points out, Club Med at Nusa Dua has 'its head in a Padmasana shrine to the northeast and its genitals and bowels in the discotheque ... '

You first discovered the surreal delights of Nusa Dua during your second trip to Bali in early 1994. Once again, the bill for this journey was footed by someone else and once again your benefactor wanted something you were unable to deliver. This time, however, your circumstances and the Bali you experienced were very different.

In 1994, you worked on a big city newspaper writing court and crime stories. You still hadn't been anywhere except Bali but you'd just booked a smoking seat to Amsterdam and were about to spend three months backpacking through Europe on $40 a day and a single pair of jeans. You liked to think the worldliness was already setting in.

Junkets like the one to Bali were doled out as part of your paper's carrot and stick approach to wrangling staff. You were being rewarded for your work on a gruelling investigation into allegations of abuse at a 1940s children's home run by a lingerie magnate hoping to create a vegetarian super race. The trip was courtesy of Ansett, the Australian airline due to crash-land seven years down the track. Ansett's media rep wanted newspaper stories about luxury Bali. Everyone knew about budget backpacker Bali, she said as you and seven other journalists gathered in Ansett's business class lounge at Sydney airport. But how many Australians knew about private plunge-pool Bali? Beachside golfcourse Bali? Thirteen-hundred-dollar-a-night royal suite where Mick Jagger once stayed Bali? *Well?*

You were keen to commence your education.

Unlike your first trip to Bali, you didn't read a thing before your departure. You were vaguely aware of the Dili massacre, of that terrible Tuesday when Indonesian troops opened fire on student protestors, slaughtering 271 and wounding hundreds more. But crime reporting required a fish-eyed focus on the urban. The drunk girl gang-raped and crushed by a government truck. The fisherman making tearful media pleas after murdering his pregnant wife. The alcoholic who killed his defacto because she wouldn't let him watch the footy. These were the horrors that kept you awake at night. Dili seemed too much like politics and not enough like crime, though later you realised this faux distinction played right into the palm of the dictator.

The Ansett trip was short and fraught – a relentless roundabout of five-star restaurants, celebrity hotel rooms and airconditioned craft shops without a single randy pig or cock-heavy cherub in sight. It was your first experience of luxury travel and you were floored by the river gorge views, the snake-and-ladder pools and the Caravaggio fruit bowls beside the bathtubs. It was certainly the first time you'd ever seen a bed three pillows wide. But something about it left you cold. Maybe it was the constant hangovers and indigestion. Maybe the absence of jungle-trekking, insect-eating and heartbreak chess. Either way, it felt like there was a thick, plastic sheath between you and everything you touched.

Instead of writing a shiny tribute to luxury Bali like the Ansett woman wanted, you began work on a cynical piece about how Bali's only charm was its weirdness. Try some live music at the government-owned Grand Bali Beach Hotel at Sanur, you suggested, sniggering at the grinning Balinese ukulele trio in glistening red shirts and gold-trimmed cowboy hats singing 'Achy Breaky Heart'. Try the toilet paper, you guffawed, pointing out that the Balinese called it *special service tissue* and enjoyed a brand called Successful. Try white-water rafting down the Ayung River in Ubud, you wrote, cacking yourself at the number of rich tourists making the bumpy eleven-kilometre trip in ironed linen shorts, designer sandals and open coffin-strength make-up. The white-water rafting was actually pretty damn exciting but you couldn't understand why anyone would travel to a foreign country to do something so culturally nonspecific. 'You'd like it better after heavy rain,' a safety dude who pronounced his name Arm A Rootin said while fitting your daggy blue helmet. 'That way you'd get more of a disco ride.'

Back at Nusa Dua, a hotel manager hosted a lunchtime banquet in Ansett's honour, offering you front-row seats at a traditional trance dance called the *Kecak*. The *Kecak* had been your favourite of all the Balinese grooves but in the middle of the Nusa Dua version, the monkey god stopped to shake hands with tourists and give the thumbs up at clicking cameras. Appalled, you cursed all cultural contamination and spent the rest of the afternoon sunburning yourself into human tempura and attempting to ingest your own body weight in Bintang at a drinking den called The Fun Pub.

The next day, when the Ansett tour bus pulled up outside yet another upmarket silversmith's, you refused to disembark and sat glowering at the hawkers milling around the bus with their shops on their heads. You shook your head but they kept pressing sarongs and woodcarvings against the bus windows. 'Fuck this island,' you wrote in a postcard to your new boyfriend back in Sydney. 'It's a piece of shit with a price-tag.' You wondered when you'd become so jaded and remembered the smashed skull of the drunk girl and the snotty tears of the killer fisherman back on the Sydney crime beat.

The following day you met Dusana. It happened when you and the rest of Team Ansett were hunkered down in Nusa Dua for *Nyepi* – the Balinese Hindu ritual marking the end of the old year and the birth of the new. The idea of *Nyepi* is to wake the evil spirits and then play dead for a day so the demons will decide Bali isn't so much fun after all and nick off to someone else's island. On the night before, giant effigies of monsters and witches called *ogoh-ogohs* are mardi gras-ed through the streets before being torched on bonfires. The 24 hours of stillness and meditation begins at midnight. Planes are grounded; cooking, driving and using electricity are forbidden; and rocks are thrown at the rooves of houses whose lights are still on. Anyone caught outside risks getting stoned the hard, painful way.

You were delighted that none of the *Nyepi* no-nos were lifted for tourists but noted that compromises were made for the island's Muslim minority. In 1994, *Nyepi* was moved because the Hindu day of silence coincided with a Muslim ceremony which involved taking to the streets and making a great deal of noise. Back then, you found it only mildly surprising that a religion practised by only about 5 per cent of the island's three million people had the power to change the date of New Year's Eve. It wasn't until much later that you — like so many other Australians visiting Bali — became aware of the awful potential for trouble between South-East Asia's only Hindu haven and the rest of Indonesia, home to 228 million Muslims and the world's most populous Islamic nation.

After a beery night of *ogoh-ogohs* on New *Nyepi*'s Eve, you spent the day of silence lounging around the curvy swimming pools in your hotel's VIP wing, eating peeled rambutans and drinking lychee daiquiris the size of mortar bombs. Next to you on the line of hotel sun-beds was a fried blonde in a string bikini with silver threads and rhinestones. Her huge sunglasses glittered and her green eye-shadow caked. She looked like she'd stepped straight out of Eurovision. 'Rich bitch,' you thought to yourself. And then you noticed she was reading *If On a Winter's Night a Traveller*.

Italo Calvino's postmodern novel about reading novels was a favourite. You loved its drastically discontinuous narrative, its deconstruction of authorial objectivity and its odd use of the second person. When you realised this was what lay between the rich bitch's sculpted fingernails you couldn't help yourself and asked, somewhat tipsily, what she thought of it. Dusana turned toward you in slow motion, sliding her gay boy blinkers down her nose and failing to focus a pair of bloodshot eyes. The book was all right, she said in a thick accent, but she preferred *Mr Palomar* (another exquisite Calvino novel addressing the ethics of the gaze in relation to naked bosoms on deserted beaches). Dusana stared at you for a moment longer, then asked if you wanted a martini.

Dusana was loaded. Her old-money English husband had died six months earlier and left her everything. Since the funeral in London, she'd mourned in Sicily, Jamaica, Hawaii, New York and now Bali. She wasn't sure where she'd grieve next but planned to leave for Singapore the day after *Nyepi*. Something about having to see a man about a lawyer.

The two of you drank more mortar bombs, slurring about writing and religion and whether anyone should ever be allowed to wear jewellery on their swimwear. (Dusana said she hadn't even noticed.) You told her about the disco ride and she told you about the spa in her suite. 'You should try it sometime,' she said, eye-shadow melting in the sun. 'It will make that white-water raft seem like resting.' A few hours later, on her big, white bed, she called out in Czech and wrapped her perfect manicure around your throat.

By the time you left her sleeping, it was twilight. Thanks to the coconut tree rule, the resort sprawled outwards instead of upwards, making navigation difficult at the best of times. With the lights dimmed for *Nyepi*, it was almost impossible and you wandered in circles for hours through acres of gloomy pools, burning torches and cement statues wearing sarongs. Eventually you ran into a young man with traditional clothes and a huge knife, one of the special guards employed to protect the resort during *Nyepi*. As he steered you towards your room, he kept clasping his hands together and saying, 'Australia and Balinese are *like this*. Very friendly.'

'Whatever,' you thought, feeling the hangover already setting in.

Back in your room, you rang your boyfriend in Sydney and told him you'd spent the afternoon reading by the pool. After hanging up, you made sure your lights were low and your curtains were drawn so the demons wouldn't know you were at home in the darkness. You dug a nest in your six-pack of pillows and thought about the Czech proverb Dusana had written inside the front cover of your journal: 'Every cat is black at night.' You tried guilt but didn't feel a thing.

—

Twelve years later, the Check Bomb driver taking you back to the Nusa Dua hotel wants to know why you're checking into such a romantic place all by yourself. He wants to know why you don't have children. Why you haven't brought a husband to help carry your mega case. You tell him you're divorced and prefer dogs, which turns out to be the funniest thing he's heard all day. 'You have dogs? *In your house?*' He makes you laugh, too. Since your first visit, Balinese locals have become very sensitive about the whole 'p' instead of 'f' and 'v' thing. The Check Bomb driver is particularly self-conscious and overcompensates by saying he'll be *farking* his car near those *feeple* over there.

You can't afford to return to the hotel's VIP wing and instead unpack in a mid-range room with a plastic torch bolted to the wall beside the desk and nasty little bottles of luminous carrot shampoo in the bathroom. Hidden in a drawer beside the bed is a sticker with a star and crescent moon pointing to Mecca. Amazingly enough, it's the first time you've ever seen any physical evidence that Bali might have Muslims and you wonder whether the extraordinarily low profile of the island's permanent Islamic population has anything to do with the explosive activities of militant visitors from the Indonesian mainland. Visitors such as Ali Amrozi bin Haji Nurhasyim, the 'smiling assassin' awaiting death for his part in the 2002 Kuta bombings.

The absence of tourists in Nusa Dua is even creepier than it was in Candidasa. In Candidasa, broke local business folk simply pack up their shops and return to the fishing boats. There are things to do and reasons to exist aside from tourism. Nusa Dua, however, is haemorrhaging – drained of the sole purpose of its existence. The submerged pool bar where you drank cocktails with Dusana is deserted. The empty beach has more security guards than suntanners. There's no competition for the beachside tables at the breakfast buffet and the iron cauldron of deep fried potato 'supper patty' remains untouched. Ask the staff about occupancy rates and they laugh with that indefatigable gallows humour. 'Low,' they grin. 'Very low.' Twenty-nine per cent is the official figure from the front desk, but the gardeners and the wait staff say this is crap. They say it's 14 per cent on a good day.

At night, you wander along the beachside promenade which runs for kilometres past abandoned resort after abandoned resort. To your right are uninhabited restaurants. To your left, grey waves breaking far out at sea. After a while, you come across a raised platform with a table set for an elaborate feast. There are origamied gold napkins beside lines of cutlery, trees draped with green fluorescent tubing and a contact number for the resort ready to host your 'royal romantic dinner'. The table looks frozen in time, as if it was melodramatically abandoned by panicked diners fleeing UFOs or giant lizards. A little further along, the track swerves inwards and you walk into a four-piece Balinese band singing 'Are You Lonesome Tonight' at a middle-aged couple waltzing alone on the sand in front of yet another empty bar.

Back at your resort's main restaurant, you browse through the Euro-Bali hybrids on the menu and order a milky daiquiri with a glace cherry the waitress is offended you don't eat. The restaurant has four musicians whose sublime harmonies do not make up for their lack of sensitivity to personal space issues. The restaurant has thousands of empty square metres they could use as a stage, but they crowd around your table bawling 'My Way' by Frank Sinatra and 'With or Without You' by U2 only centimetres from your face. You try to concentrate on your food but this is a mistake, too. The minestrone is viscous, like warm, brown Clag, and comes with a dollop of chilli pesto and rock-hard kidney beans. The spaghetti omelet is only slightly better. The band asks if there's anything you'd like to hear and you nominate 'The Sound of Silence'. They play it with a Latin beat and a chorus of bawdy olés.

At dawn the next morning, you return to the beachside track and watch hundreds of path-sweepers and pool-cleaners beautify grounds only they will admire. Every night, bits of Bali fall into the pools and every morning they are sifted clean. Beachcombers smooth the sand on the beaches with long rakes in the hope that someone will come to make footprints. Signs at the borders between hotels say you will be searched but the security guards seem lethargic and depressed. A German power-walker surges past with huge weights strapped to his ankles, wrists and back. A bulging man in hibiscus boardshorts grabs at a Balinese squirrel in a palm tree. High up on the balcony of one of the uglier resorts is a Japanese business-man standing on his verandah and gazing out to sea. He's wearing a black dinner suit. It is 6.30 a.m.

On the last day of your trip to Bali in 1994, you and the rest of Team Ansett spent the day on a yacht cruising water the colour of novelty contact lenses. Around lunchtime you spotted the crab – a large, nippery bugger riding a hot-pink rubber thong that pitched wildly about in your wake. For some reason you found the sight intoler-ably troubling. One of your travelling companions ridiculed you for worrying about the fate of a single crustacean while you simultaneously inhaled large chunks of satayed picnic cow, but you didn't care. You tried desperately to swish the crusty day-tripper towards the dubious safety of the yacht, but the current worked against you and the more you swished, the further the crab drifted away. You caught one last glimpse of its beady little eyes as both it and the pink thong were mowed down by a speedboat towing a giant, tourist-laden inflatable banana. It was horrible. It was just a crab on a thong, but it was horrible. There was something about the absurd helplessness of the victim and the crassness of the assassin that was indescribably disturbing.

When you eventually published your story about weird Bali, you wrote about the crab and said the only survival skill worth learning in the Byron Bay of Indonesia was the ability to avoid other tourists. If someone had told you there'd be a time when you'd miss the tourist hordes and when human day-trippers would also be obliterated by indiscriminate assassins, you would have told them they were dreaming.

FIVE

Honeymoon Price

Four years after the Ansett trip you married a Brisbane rock star you barely knew. You met at a dinner party thrown by a women's magazine and fell in love over email. He proposed the night your newspaper sent you on a raw lobster-eating date with One Nation's David Oldfield and, despite having always vowed never to say 'I do', you said you would.

The wedding was in an inner-city pub early one Sunday morning. You exchanged vows across a beer barrel in front of friends, family and a couple of old gutter blokes who'd come to at the sound of the bridal Valiant's exhaust pipes scraping along the asphalt. In the gift stack was a fire extinguisher, a banana slicer and a $20 Woolworths voucher. Your new mother-in-law sang 'Crazy' by Patsy Cline with the wedding band, and you danced until your heels were minced, absolutely euphoric.

Marrying a guitar-playing stranger had its drawbacks. The day after the wedding, he returned to the road and his manager told you girlfriends weren't allowed on tour. Three months passed before you were able to book the honeymoon and by then you were no longer eligible for the newlywed packages with the freebie fruit bowls and the sticky bottles of sparkling wine. You decided to go to Bali because it was easy and offered cheap rooms at short notice.

The budget flight over was infested with newlyweds. Behind you was a pair of elderly love birds taking a second bite of the marital pie – and of each other's jowly throats. You vowed to die before you got old as one or other of the pashing pensioners (in their position it was impossible to tell who was who) took a loud slurp at what sounded very much like an armpit. In the seats in front were twenty-something honeymoon archetypes who'd been dating since high school and had finally decided to tie the knot. Bum-bagged and suffering murderous nicotine withdrawal, Cheryl and Bruce sat separated by a spare seat, breaking the silence only to fight over who'd had the passports last and whether or not duty-free French perfume really did contain essence of genuine cat's testicle.

At the airport in Denpasar, you and your tousled new mate fought off several smaller, weaker newlyweds in the cat-fight for cabs before driving to the Hotel Tjampuhan in Ubud. Built in 1928 for guests of the Prince of Ubud, this extraordinary establishment hangs off the side of a stunning jungle gorge at the juncture of the Oos and Tjam-puhan rivers just outside of Ubud. It came to prominence in 1934 when it became the starting point for an artists' association founded by, among others, Walter Spies. According to Adrian Vickers, this aristocratic German intellectual was a sensitive and reclusive young man seeking a homosexual paradise away from the strict social mores of Europe. Vickers notes that in Bali back then, homosexuality was not a matter for moral condemnation but simply a pastime for young unmarried men.

Spies' private predilections have been expunged from most Indonesian-generated accounts of his life in much the same way that Jack Twist's love-sick pleas to his cowboy lover were erased from the pirate copy of *Brokeback Mountain*. Yet when you and the rock star checked in at the Hotel Tjampuhan, you discovered that Spies' former house was a central attraction and that the hotel's decorative theme was decidedly venereal. The main pool, for instance, was surrounded by a brazen frieze of anatomically correct stone monkeys in a range of sexual positions that made the Kama Sutra look as tame as an IKEA instruction sheet. 'What's that little monkey doing to that big monkey?' a frying child asked his casseroling mother down by the pool. 'Well,' she replied – shortly before disappearing beneath a stampede of Australian honeymooners who'd stripped the dinner buffet like locusts – 'when two monkeys, or in this case, two hundred monkeys, love each other very much … '

The sweaty bell-hop, meanwhile, had just discovered the two of you were honeymooners and could no longer contain himself. 'You got a snake in here?' he asked your husband as he lugged your bags to the room. 'It's heavy enough, maaaayte.' Then, in a hideously lascivious whisper: 'Honeymoon, eh? You want some hot gamelan music for the bedroom? You gonna make some sons here in Bali? You gonna get some tonight, ay maaaayte … ?'

After a long day of international travel, making anything was out of the question. But the bell-hop refused to give in. 'Remember tonight,' he whispered as he slunk off into the humidity. 'Remember tonight.' That's when you noticed the red, wooden demon dangling beside the hotel room door. It had a Mohican of stiff black hair, an expression of either unspeakable agony or incomparable ecstasy and, rising between two mounds of splintery wood serving as thighs, what looked very much like an enormous detachable wooden phallus.

The next morning you asked the breakfast woman about the demon. She removed the tray of banana pancakes from her head and looked at you as if you were an absolute idiot. As if you'd just asked what one plus one was, or whether or not it was a good idea to give Megawati Sukarnoputri a shot at the presidential title. (Indonesia's future leader was very popular in Bali at the time. Apart from having family connections on the island, Megawati gained sympathy among the Balinese when her opponents tried to thwart her political career by accusing her of being Hindu.)

'It's a bell,' the breakfast lady said in a 'duh' voice. She grabbed the demon and wrenched out its wedding tackle with a grip that would have left any ordinary bloke rolling round the floor weeping Bee Gees tunes. 'You bang it like this if you want room service.' And as she used the demon's cock to thump away on its ribs, you noticed that every Hotel Tjampuhan bungalow – each packed refugee-style with Australian honeymooners – had a bell just like yours. 'Well, not just like yours,' the breakfast woman added. 'Each has a different tone so I know which room is calling. Now eat your pancakes. You need to keep up your strength if you're going to make some sons here in Bali.'

During the week you spent in Ubud, smirking locals made jokes about whether or not you were busy making sons more times than they offered you transport, sarongs and marijuana. This was a lot of times. Unfortunately your answers were not to their satisfaction and before long an advertisement for Viagra USA ('delivered to your hotel within the hour') was thoughtfully deposited in your room. You responded by banging for room service far more frequently than was necessary.

Desperate to avoid this obsession with honeymoon son-making, you tried masquerading as regular tourists. You rode 100cc motorbikes to an elephant safari park which displayed a Kevin Bloody Wilson signature in a frame. You dropped by a budget cremation and watched a fat man flame by the side of a main road. You laughed at the restaurant menu which recommended *checking your teets* before eating Balinese duck.

'For you, special morning price,' the hawkers flogging baseball caps and cocaine shouted. 'For you, special afternoon price. Special business price. Special sunset price.' Then, with a suspicious glance sideways: 'Hold on. You sure you two don't want special honeymoon price?'

Weary of all the attention, you packed your bags and headed south to the shit-fight that was Kuta. Back in Australia, the travel agent had insisted your three-and-a-bit-star beach resort would be the lap of luxury. In reality, however, it was the lap of low rentedness. The beach was murky, the airconditioner clunked and all the in-house movies had been pirated the old-fashioned way – via shysters holding unsteady video cameras in movie theatres. One of the gangster cinematographers responsible for the selection in your room had a particularly dark sense of humour and could be heard cackling loudly through the saddest, slowest moments of *Meet Joe Black*. The brutalised soundtrack revealed he was also a keen nose-blower, chest-cougher and phlegm-gargler.

Outside, the resort's pool bar was dominated by a

phalanx of German bachelors whose chain-drinking of Bintang beer was not accompanied by suitably frequent visits to the lavatory. The beach was full of newly retired (or newly operated on) Europeans letting it all hang out in G-strings or, in some harrowing cases, no strings at all. Then there were all the Australian honeymooners. Down by the sea and the sunsets, there were enough of them to start up some sort of super race – a brave new breed you hoped would soon become extinct thanks to an excess of necking while doused in toxic, tropical-strength insect repellent.

By the time you flew home in matching Hawaiian-style shirts, you and the rock star were sunburned, irritable and feeling just that little bit more like Cheryl and Bruce from the plane trip over. In three years, the son-less marriage would be over.

—

When you return to the Hotel Tjampuhan in 2006, the first thing you notice is that the hordes of Australian honeymooners have been replaced by a polite handful of Japanese honeymooners. The second thing you notice is that despite Jakarta's escalating modesty campaigns, the fornicating monkey frieze and the room bells with the telescopic timber tonks are still alive and leering.

Bali has always been schizophrenic when it comes to sex – split between outsider fantasies of tropical island sauciness and the modest reality of a culture and religion so conservative that, even today, only 2 or 3 per cent of Balinese women engage in (or at least own up to engaging in) sex outside marriage. That said, Balinese culture has a yogic flexibility when it comes to accommodating tourist culture. Guidebooks advise backpackers to consume only moderate amounts of alcohol to avoid scandalising the locals while signs outside Ubud pubs bawl, *Get yourself drunk!* The Lonely Planet guide tells travellers to cover their knees, shoulders and armpits yet Bali used to boast one of the world's only escort agencies for women. For $1600 a night, Escorts in Paradise offered discerning ladies the company of a guy billed as having it all.

Complicating the situation now is Jakarta's hardline Muslim campaign to introduce elements of Islamic law into Indonesia's legal system. The notorious Anti-Pornography and Pornographic Acts Bill was revived in 2005 after Susilo Bambang Yudhoyono became disturbed by the sight of women's navels and erotic dancing on telly. Of particular concern to Indonesian conservatives were the bump and grindings of pop singer Inul Daratista, whose name translates roughly as 'she of the boobs'.

In 2006, a special government committee was appointed to hear public submissions on the new legislation in an attempt to clarify exactly what sorts of behaviour constituted 'porno action' and were capable of 'arousing lust in children'. If passed in its current form, the bill will ban depictions of nudity in the media and the arts. People who kiss in public, shack up while unmarried, have homo sex, view erotic displays, or flash a sensual body part such as a thigh, buttock, breast or navel, could spend up to ten years in the slammer and be fined more than $A100,000.

Committee chairman Balkan Kaplale (from Yudhoyono's own Democratic Party) maintains that the legislation will have prophylactic potential against natural disasters. He says that the South-East Asian tsunami – as well as recent landslides and earthquakes – are warnings from God about the immorality accompanying Indonesia's era of reform. After the May 2006 earthquake in Java, the citizens of devastated Yogyakarta seemed to agree. 'Allah is angry with his people and the country's leaders,' one villager told reporters. 'This was a warning.'

As Yudhoyono deflects criticism that he is pandering to Islamic hardliners in his parliament, local governments have jumped on the anti-jiggy jig bandwagon and introduced Sharia on the sly via harsh morality bylaws. In the city of Tanggerang on the outskirts of Jakarta, the onus is on women found alone at night to prove they aren't whores. Lilies Lindawati, a pregnant mother of two, breached this defacto curfew in February 2006. She was waiting for a bus at 8 p.m. when five public order officials accused her of being a sex worker and forced her into the back of a van. Imprisoned and denied permission to call her teacher husband, she was tried the next day in a makeshift tent with 26 other women. Lindawati pleaded not guilty but the judge said the face powder and lipstick in her handbag proved she was a prostitute and not a housewife. Tanggerang's newest hooker was unable to pay the $34 fine and spent three days in jail.

These crackdowns on Indonesia's scourge of seductresses are supported by thuggish militant groups such as the Islamic Defenders Front which has trashed bars and stoned the offices of Indonesia's *Playboy* magazine (the publishers of which put out one heavily clothed, heavily de-nippled edition before going into hiding). But critics say the anti-pornography bill threatens artists and cultural diversity. Between 80 and 90 per cent of Indonesians identify as Muslims, yet the nation has hundreds of ethnic groups, many of which sport Islamically unsound dress codes. On West Papua, for instance, women often get about bare-breasted while the chaps prefer penis gourds (some of which are up to half a metre long and are used to store additional, non-anatomical valuables such as cigarettes and money). Indonesian feminist groups are also appalled. 'Women here have always dressed sexily and in tight clothes, this law is something very alien to us,' university professor Gadis Arriva has said. '[The new law] states it is illegal to express any sexual desire, even to imagine sex. How do you prove that?'

Bali, meanwhile, is so concerned about the bill's effect on its culture and bikini-led tourism industry that some officials and activists have threatened to secede if the island is not exempted from the new rules. This seems an unlikely proposition but suggests Indonesia's notorious obsession with maintaining sovereignty over its 18,108 islands could become increasingly untenable if it attempts to enforce religious or cultural homogeneity. When central government legislators arrived in Bali to gauge local reaction in March 2006, they were greeted by a thousand protestors defending the island's 'cultural sensuality'. These activists included traditional dance groups, artists and farmers, as well as cheerleaders, transsexuals, punk rockers and G-string-wearing gyrators. One elderly dancer earned wild applause after tossing away her top and performing a traditional *joged bumbung* dance bare-breasted. A local performance poet followed suit and removed an article of clothing with each stanza.

'Balinese arts and religious beliefs have never considered sensuality and sexuality as an impure, morally reprehensible thing,' rally organiser Cok Sawitri told the press. 'Instead, sensuality and sexuality are treated as natural, integral parts of our lives as human beings. In the past, Balinese women never wore a bra, yet the custom did not turn the society into a sex-craving, pornographically demented community.'

The Tjampuhan Hotel's new alfresco spa isn't

pornographically demented but it is extremely nude. After unpacking alone in a honeymoon suite full of hibiscus flowers and memories, you book in for a two-hour traditional massage and are led to a room carved out of rock in the steep cliff leading down to the river. The only protection from the elements – and the eyes of a group of male bathers just down the hill – is a plastic shower curtain, but the massage chick pulls this aside after asking you to strip. Once again, you remember the guidebook's promises about the cloak of invisibility and once again you note the emperor-style shortfallings of this cloak as the river men begin quietly woo hoo-ing. After a rigorous pummeling, the masseuse mortar and pestles up a paste of nutmeg, turmeric, cloves, white pepper and ginger before basting you like a stick of chicken satay and leaving you to marinate.

Like everyone who finds out you're Australian, the clerk behind the counter at reception wants to know where the hell you've all gone. 'Ah yes,' he sighs, before you can answer. 'After bomb Bali two triple warning.' Only thirteen out of the Tjampuhan's 67 rooms are occupied and the clerk warns that the hourly shuttle-bus schedule to Ubud is no longer quite so hourly. 'Ring if you are feeling a little bit urgent,' he suggests.

You walk kilometers up the hill into town and return to the monkey forest where you chat with a guide about the Ubud youth scene. The guide says too many young people aren't familiar with their native tongues, but that he's keeping his Balinese language in a safe place so it doesn't get lost. (Bahasa Bali, the local language, is very different to Bahasa Indonesia, the national version. The former is far more complex, has completely different vocabulary and grammar and takes various forms relating to traditional caste systems.) Asked how Balinese youth feel about

Jakarta, the monkey guide pauses: 'Have you ever noticed that when you ask the Balinese where they're from they say Bali and not Indonesia?' A monstrous monkey carrying a Coke can climbs onto your head and abseils down your back. 'Sit calmly and you'll be fine,' the guide says. You follow his instructions but are not fine at all. The monkey pokes at your face then viciously sinks its teeth into your left buttocks. The guide has watched tourists get bitten by monkeys so many times before, he can no longer be bothered laughing. 'Oh well,' he says as you run from the forest clutching what you are convinced is a rabies-positive bottom cheek, 'obviously you weren't calm enough.'

You bolt into the nearest bathroom and yank down your trousers, twisting and turning in front of the mirror in an attempt to work out whether your skin has been pierced. It hasn't and you wonder whether you were saved by your ultra-thick, ultra-daggy, Bridget Jones-style underwear – like that blonde from the women's magazines who was shot in the chest but saved by her silicon boobs.

Back on the main drag, you are almost mowed down by a petrol tanker spray-painted with a mural of screaming skulls, top-hatted skeletons, Asian mystics and a topless chick nursing a baby. Big letters across the windscreen read: *God Bless*. You pass an advertising billboard of a beaming woman pulling out her hair. Graffiti reading *Fuck N Area*. A mangy-looking live chicken tied by the leg to a pirate DVD shop. You see a couple of Australian-looking tourists but these turn out to be Dutch and American. Everyone else is Japanese. Australians, it seems, really have heeded the bomb Bali two triple warning.

The sun goes down and you cross a long, unlit footbridge in pitch blackness, nearly plunging through one of the many missing planks into the river below. You stop for dinner at a restaurant and order a special Balinese chicken dish that comes with an *egg plan*. The waiter offers you Disco Peanuts which contain salt and sugar in equally inedible quantities and make you retch when combined with the clouds of diesel fumes rolling in from the road outside. You return to your room and fail to sleep, convinced food poisoning, monkey disease and killer earthquakes are nigh.

The next morning, two men arrive to make up your room and change the hibiscus flowers. The larger of the two asks if you slept well and you tell him no, you had nightmares. 'Call your family immediately,' he suggests, sounding worried. Before you can ask him to explain, he launches into a speech about how the next time you have bad dreams, you must get up and wash your feet and face. Nightmares come from the past but can only enter through the feet and the back of the head, he says. After the dream lesson, he replaces the wilted hibiscus blossoms with new ones that will also be dead by tomorrow. He takes the liberty of putting flowers behind your ears while you're sitting writing, telling you to look in the mirror to see how beautiful, how Balinese you've become.

The smaller of the two cleaners sees a photo of your dogs on your computer and asks how much they weigh, nodding approvingly when you say the largest clocks in at 30 kilos. He says he has two children, a boy and a girl, but has run out of money to have more. When you tell him you're writing a book about Australians visiting Bali, he drops his broom and grabs your arm. 'Please help us!' he cries. The bigger man shoots him a look and the smaller man releases his grip and leaves.

'Sorry,' he says.

But it's you who feels you should apologise.

SIX

Harm's Way

It was the little details that were most disturbing about that first bombing in Bali. Sure the big picture was horrific: buildings razed, hundreds dead, profound regional and international ramifications. But in the searing heat of the moment, nothing could compete with the one miserable hero who tried to rescue a girl from the disco inferno and had to leave her behind when he realised her back was split in half.

It was testimony to the vast scale of the tragedy that these monstrous minutiae appeared almost as afterthoughts in media coverage. You had to read long and hard to discover the volunteer in the grotesquely overwhelmed Graha Asih Hospital who used curtains as bandages while the place flooded with 'blood, vomit and piss'. Or the Victorian holidaymaker who came to under a pile of bodies and was repeatedly electrocuted as he tried to pull himself free. Or the woman with the punctured stomach, the legless man trying to drag himself to safety, the charcoaled hand severed as it made a last snatch for help.

This is the bloody reality that journalistic shorthand such as 'bomb blast' airbrushes out.

The night two ammonium nitrate bombs obliterated Paddy's Bar and the Sari Club in Kuta on 12 October 2002 was dubbed Australia's September 11. Of the 202 corpses, 88 were Australian – ordinary Aussie tourists whose prosaic pleasure-seeking was deemed to be 'immoral' by the bombing conspirators. There was also a third explosion outside Bali's American consulate. This device didn't cause serious injury or damage but was packed with excrement, sending an unmistakable 'fuck you' to the West. As academics debated whether the second front of the global war on terrorism would be South-East Asia, Australia reeled at the realisation that it had become a target, mourning not only the slaughter of its innocents but the loss of its exotic holiday sanctuary. As Richard White and Ingrid Bown put it:

> The media aestheticised the bombings in their curiously poetic tabloid way, evoking a sense of bewilderment and betrayal at paradise lost ... The bombs 'forever destroyed our innocence'... [and] a kind of emotional imperialism took hold. Bali was imagined as an Australian possession ... Childhood innocence was evoked in descriptions of the island as Australia's 'playground' or 'backyard' ... The place to which they had entrusted their images of paradise and freedom for safekeeping should have been inviolable.

Incredibly enough, tourism in Bali soon bounced back: 1.46 million tourists arrived in 2004 compared to 1.42 million before the bombing. This was partly due to an Australian perception that returning to Bali with outstretched arms and bulging wallets was a moral responsibility. As travel writer Michael Gebicki wrote in the *Sun-Herald* in October 2003:

> Spend, spend, spend. It doesn't have to be lavish … So go ahead, have a beach massage, buy another sarong or a T-shirt from those pesky beach vendors, a musical bamboo windmill for the garden or another helping of sticky black rice and you'll be doing everyone a favour.

The hedonistic Bali holiday experience had become altruistic, a charitable endeavour offering secular salvation to the struggling local citizens.

Australia's protective and somewhat paternalistic new attitude to Indonesia was epitomised by its munificent response to the 2004 Boxing Day tsunami. The Australian government's $1 billion aid package set records and matched the largesse of its populace. In fact, the generosity of individual Australians was so great that Médecins sans Frontières had to offer to return donations after receiving four times the 20 million needed to fund its response to the disaster after only three days of international appeals.

Eight months later, all the goodwill evaporated. The culprit was former Gold Coast beauty student Schapelle Corby who was caught at Denpasar airport with 4.1 kilograms of marijuana in her now infamous boogie-board bag. Corby was found guilty of drug-smuggling and sentenced to twenty years' jail. Minutes after the verdict, Australia exploded. Corby's supporters were convinced someone had let their girl down. Public enemy number one was the Indonesian justice system and its 'monkey' judges. Other fashionable villains included John Howard (because he'd failed to force Indonesia's independent judges to implement a more preferable verdict), Qantas baggage handlers dressed in stolen camel suits (because they'd probably planted the dope in the first place) and recipients of tsunami aid in Aceh (because those selfish bastards were too busy tending mass graves to make a single court submission).

It was the height of unfashionability to suggest that the person who let Corby down might have been Corby herself.

Opinion polls showed that more than 90 per cent of Australians believed her innocent and many punters complained bitterly about sentencing disparity in Indonesian courts. Comparisons were made between Corby's lengthy jail term and the two-year sentence served by the radical Indonesian cleric, Abu Bakar Ba'asyir – widely regarded as the mastermind of the Bali bombings (though this was never proved in court). Perhaps the most infamous case of Indonesian demonisation was when Sydney radio announcer Malcolm T. Elliott called Indonesia's president and the case judges banana-eating apes. Elliott was sacked from 2GB after saying, 'The judges don't even speak English, mate, they're straight out of the trees … '

Team Corby encouraged the nation to cancel holidays to Bali and boycott Indonesian products. Actor Russell Crowe was one of many who said Indonesia should show some appreciation for Australia's tsunami aid package. The protests took an ominous turn when two bullets were sent to the Indonesian consulate in Perth accompanied by a letter warning that staff would be killed unless Corby was released. Then a white powder containing a 'biological agent' was mailed to the Indonesian embassy in Canberra. While the powder was found to be harmless, the incident saw the embassy closed and more than forty staff undergo a decontamination process. It received worldwide coverage and made front-page news across Indonesia. Fears of an anti-Australian backlash were so great, a water cannon was set up outside the Australian embassy in Jakarta.

This wasn't the first time Australia and Indonesia's fragile rapport threatened to unravel. Political, cultural and economic differences had always stymied bilateral ties between the big, white, wealthy Western continent and the impoverished, Islamic archipelago. The relationship was marked by peaks and troughs, hitting a low in 1999 when Australia backed East Timor in its battle for independence. But after an initial coldness toward Asia, John Howard began working hard to build a relationship with Susilo Bambang Yudhoyono. The president affectionately known as SBY also made many conciliatory gestures to overcome the 'mutual distrust and antagonism' of the past. Howard and SBY remained upbeat about their bilateral bonds even after the almighty diplomatic row over Australia's decision to grant protection visas to 42 West Papuan asylum seekers in January 2006.

Ordinary Australians and Indonesians, however, have always been far more ambivalent. Numerous studies – including surveys done for the Australian Strategic Policy Institute, the Ipsos Mackay Report and the Australia–Indonesia Institute – reveal an enduring Australian fear and distrust of Indonesia. By the same token, many Indonesians remain resentful about East Timor and are unaware of the extent of Australia's tsunami aid commitment. SBY has the added difficulty of a splintered parliament and anti-Australian elements within Indonesia's political and military elite – not to mention the inflammatory oratory of religious leaders such as Abu Bakar Ba'asyir who's advised John Howard to convert to Islam if he wants to avoid a fiery incineration in hell.

The Indonesian public's reaction to the Corby case has also been telling. Despite claims by Corby's mother that Bali was in shock at her daughter's sentence, the initial Indonesian reaction seemed to be either disinterest or bemusement. After Australia's hysteria escalated, however, many Indonesian commentators criticised Australian irrationalism, emotionalism, racism and cultural cluelessness. There were also charges of hypocrisy given the nation's past lobbying for Indonesian courts to act free of political influence. Protesters gathered at the Australian embassy in Jakarta calling for Corby to receive the death sentence and carrying placards reading: *Corby drug dealer must die.*

Australian enthusiasm for the case waned as time passed and as unsavoury revelations were made about Corby's history and drug-tainted family. By the time the grungy mugs of the Bali Nine first flashed across Australian television screens, the nation had well and truly reached compassion fatigue. These nine young Australians were arrested in Denpasar in April 2005 for trying to smuggle $A4 million worth of heroin. Since then, ringleaders Andrew Chan and Myuran Sukumaran have been sentenced to death via firing squad. Also awaiting execution are Matthew Norman, Scott Rush, Tach Duc Thanh Nguyen and Si Yi Chen. Martin Stephens and Michael Czugaj received a life sentence, while Renae Lawrence is serving twenty years.

Paul Toohey, an author and senior writer for the *Bulletin*, doesn't think Australians have ever cared about the Bali Nine as much as they should.

It was always said about Schapelle that people only cared about her because she was a passable spunk. Well, there's not too many spunks among the Bali Nine.

Half of them aren't even white. I always thought that people would soften if any of them were sentenced to death, let alone shot. But the poison of public opinion seems to read otherwise, at this point. People are saying: 'Good job ... '

Australians have also been cynical about Michelle Leslie, the lingerie model who served three months in Kerobokan Prison in 2005 after being caught with two ecstasy tablets in her handbag outside an open-air dance party near the seaside restaurant strip of Jimbaran Bay. Leslie was lambasted after declaring herself a Muslim and making court appearances in a head-to-toe black Muslim burqa. She strenuously denied accusations of fakery but, much later, admitted in a magazine interview that she'd been pretending all along. She said she'd veiled up to avoid being raped in jail.

In the midst of all this, the terrorists struck again. On 1 October 2005, suicide bombers detonated themselves at Jimbaran Bay and in the Raja restaurant in Kuta Square. Twenty-three people were killed (four of them Australian) and more than 120 people were injured. Police said the bombs used were different from previous blasts in that most deaths and injuries were inflicted by shrapnel, rather than chemical explosion. X-rays showed pellets and ball bearings lodged in victims' backs.

Paul Toohey was in Bali the day after the blasts and went to the morgue to look at bodies and body parts:

An Indonesian cameraman showed me some footage he had taken only fifteen minutes after Raja went up. The police had put up a cordon but asked him to come in because his camera had a powerful lamp on it. The footage showed police picking up what he called strips of 'bomber meat' – flesh that was once the suicide bomber. The cameraman said: 'Look – bomber penis.' Sure enough, there went the bomber's knob into the bucket. No balls, but, as some wag noted, he didn't have any anyway.

This time, tourism to Bali did not recover, with the number of Australian travellers falling by 60 per cent in the first quarter of 2006. 'They think it's bloody Baghdad here,' one resort owner complained to the press. Average occupancy rates are now hovering round 20 per cent for most hotels, though one local says some have dropped to 3 per cent. International air links have been cut back, mass sackings are common, and about 30 to 40 per cent of Bali's travel agents are believed to have gone bankrupt. Community leaders say the Balinese are out of hope. Asked what he thinks of the future for tourism in Bali, Toohey is blunt. 'Fucked,' he replies.

This is also a reasonable adjective to describe the way you feel after dining on yet another load of odd, Balinese hotel hybrid cuisine: pizza with a curried tomato sauce base and a toasted sandwich which arrives with cold toast, cold cheese and great wedges of cold onion. It's the last leg of your visit and you've checked into the leafy Seminyak resort where your mother and brother stayed during the family trip that wasn't in 2003.

The fight this trip was supposed to mend was a shocker. Your mother's side of the family was meant to be the solid side, the side where everyone got along. The realisation that all this could disintegrate over something as petty as the Christmas holiday use of a computer mouse was devastating.

Not that such battles are ever really about computer accessories.

Six icy months of alienation passed before your mother proposed a reconciliation trip and the three of you settled on a long weekend in Bali. By that stage, the first bombing was just a hazy newspaper headline and you actually tried using the Australian government's longstanding 'defer all essential travel' to Bali alert as a bargaining chip with the travel agent. Then, three days before you were due to depart, another suicide bomber detonated another car bomb outside the lobby of the JW Marriott Hotel in Jakarta and another twelve people perished.

At first you were full of bravado, emailing your travelling companions an elaborate seven-point plan about why the trip should proceed. But after two nights of insomnia and visions of burning flesh, you made the sickening decision to cancel. As you drove your mother and brother to the airport, you felt like a fox that had had to eat off a leg to escape from a steel snare. You just hoped they knew the trap was your fear and not their company.

Three years later, you sprawl on the daybed your mother and brother raved about in their postcard and stare out the window into the resort's nectarous gardens. The room is huge, stunning and infested with mosquitos. Every so often an elderly woman passes by flicking water with a frangipani and topping up offerings with packets of peanuts. Imagining your family here without you makes you sad. You keep wondering, 'Would they have done this?', 'Would they have done that?'. Berating yourself again for having been too scared to join them, you vow to spend your final days here hurling yourself into harm's way.

SEVEN

Fuck Terrorists – They're Bollocks

The first dangerous thing you do is walk the streets of Kuta at dusk on a Friday night. (Not that it's bloody Baghdad or anything.) You leave Seminyak in the middle of the afternoon and walk five kilometres down the beach, past eight games of sand soccer, past sunbakers roasting next to rivulets of raw sewage, past a young monkey fighting three wild dogs and past scores of topless white men whose pecs jiggle furiously over their heart monitors as they jog damply down the beach.

Escorts in Paradise may have folded, but there are still plenty of girls' nights out advertised on big, beachside billboards. The Hard Rock Hotel offers a special deal on Wednesdays: 50 per cent off selected drinks as well as *bar dances* and *sparking body grinders*. Another venue has a promotional billboard featuring photos of young male performers who look like they're screaming in pain. Perhaps on account of all the sparking and grinding.

As you reach the main beach at Kuta, the catcalls from the gypsy hucksters increase in volume but still sound tired. *Excusememotorbike? Howlongyoubeeninbalioneweek? Lookylooky* … One beachside beautician engrossed in a game of chess yells *plaityourhairdarling?* without even bothering to look up and make eye contact. The sea next to her is a steely teal and no one hires the surfboards propped up along the road.

Kuta's narrow streets are as claustrophobic and quirky as ever. You pass businesses called Lemon Chic, Funky Princess, Rizky Leather and Executif Tailor. You pass a restaurant promising *life lobster*; a shop dedicated entirely to pink thongs with rhinestones; and an emporium selling sheets, *fillows* and *certain sandals*. It's easy to dismiss Bali's glut of consumer goods as crapulous, but they're pure class next to the plastic gismos in Australia's plague of $2 stores.

Not far from the fillows is a shifty dude selling pirate DVDs who says if you buy ten, he'll give you three for free. Next door, his shifty competitor says if you buy a hundred, she'll give you fifty. 'Business price,' she winks, stacking a mountain of *Kath and Kim* discs in her front window. It's easy to imagine the Fountain Lake flossies living it up big here, revelling in their newfound 'effluence' and marvelling at how noice, different, and unuuuuuusal everything is.

A pestering woman grabs your arm to offer you a T-shirt taking the piss out of Bali pesterers. It says: *No, I don't want a f—ing bemo, massage, postcard, plait your hair, bracelet, money belt, necklaces, magic mushroom, jiggy jig*. The pestering woman sinks her long fingers into your flesh and misses the irony completely. You say no to her pestering T-shirt as well as her *I'm a Virgin* T-shirt, her *Jiggy Jig* T-shirt and her *Show Me Your Tits* T-shirt. You refuse her friend offering VIP magic mushrooms.

In Poppies Lane you take refuge in an airconditioned

punk shop called Suicide Glam full of pretty young Asian things whose lips and septums drip with piercings and whose arms crawl with tattoos. Suicide Glam has tartan microskirts, skull handbags and a protest T-shirt that reads *Fuck Terrorists – They're Bollocks* followed by the enigmatic and somewhat contradictory *Here's Suicide Glam – Always Remains Strong*. According to the punk shop's website, this 100 per cent cotton product provides 'a full frontal message to all the stupid weak-ass terrorists'.

You purchase one of these South-East Asia meets Johnny Rotten fashion statements and walk into a cement jungle full of wilted Hindu offerings topped by what look like Arnott's biscuits. A line of schoolgirls cycle down a cement drain. A toothless guy rides a pushbike loaded with carved watermelon and pineapple. A café offers *parking in the back side*. You reach the Sari Club bomb site and stand next to a feral dog missing half its head. The dog has more open wound than skin and fur and is freaking people out. They yell and kick as they pass. You stare at the bare, grassy lot where all those backs were split and all those stomachs were punctured and find it hard to feel anything except hot, tired and sorry for the dog. Balinese authorities seem similarly bewildered by this desecrated real estate. They plan to turn it into a carpark like the site of Paddy's Bar.

Back at the beach you eat at a place offering free frog dances and bright orange pad Thai. There's a dying flower on the table and a toilet paper dispenser in the bathroom promising fresh life. Sitting next door are two Australian tourists – the first you've seen since the flight over. He's balding, she's plump, and they're both in flowery red shirts. The couple tells you they're here on their twentieth wedding anniversary and that they came because their friends kept telling them how beautiful the Balinese people were. 'Don't you agree?' the woman beams. 'Don't you think the Balinese are just the most BEAUTIFUL people?'

You've always hated the way misty-eyed Australians fat with cash go on about the beauty of the Balinese. Sure the waiters smile a lot but is there no one here who's kinda funny-looking? No one who's ever having a bad day? No one who's just a tiny bit pissed, shirty or cheesed off that the average Australian spends more on a single night's beer here than the average farmer earns in a month? You loathe the patronising simplicity of the generalisation but you're so happy to hear a familiar accent, you beam right back. 'OH YES,' you shout, face fluorescent with pad Thai. 'THEY'RE JUST THE MOST BEAUTIFUL PEOPLE EVER.'

In the cab on the way back to the hotel, the beautiful Balinese driver tries to make polite conversation about Australian topics of interest.

'Corby,' he says. 'She's free, isn't she?'

'No,' you reply. 'Maybe you're thinking of Michelle Leslie.'

'Who?' the cabbie asks. The names and faces of all those imprisoned white drug girls run together after a while.

Halfway back to the hotel you change your mind and ask the driver to drop you off at a ritzy bar and restaurant in Seminyak called Ku De Tu. You've arranged to visit Kerobokan Prison in the morning, are anticipating a sleepless night and decide you might as well spend some of it drinking campari. Seminyak has been mentioned in Australian travel advisories as one of the possible locations for future terrorist attacks and Ku De Ta – a place where tickets to premium functions can reach $340 a head – is regarded as one of the island's most tempting terrorist marks. 'Of course this is the logical target,' says Ku De Ta's marketing and promotions manager, Donni One. 'But it's also the hardest. The bombers would never get in.'

One has a point. This is the first place you've been to in Bali where the security doesn't seem just for show. Cabs aren't allowed up the long driveway and must dump their passengers beside the road. Some minibuses get special dispensation but only after a ferocious frisking by throngs of guards with automatic weapons. Your bag is searched twice on the long walk in and sentinels patrol the side perimeters and the beach with sniffer dogs and ostentatious armory.

Compared to everywhere else, Ku De Ta is packed. In fact, it's the most white people you've seen in one place since you arrived. You perch at the bar ordering over-priced campari and finger-friendly Tex Mex as scores of tourists video the sunset and listen to the DJ play Enya. The sky is crazy beautiful, alchemising the dirty beach and dirty surfers into wild pinks and golds. A beacon of light shoots toward the ocean and illuminates every moth in town.

After the light dies, you track down Donni One, a slick operator who always seems to be looking at something more interesting over your shoulder. One tells you his in-house security staff have been trained by former military and special forces experts from Australia. He then hands you a sheet detailing Ku De Ta's strategies vis-à-vis bomb recognition, personal belonging checks, criminal motive anticipation, surveillance, evacuation procedures and security ground formations. During big events, Ku De Ta has snipers on the roof. 'Not that anyone would ever know,' One says, straining over your shoulder.

Returning alone to the bar you order another campari and think about 'Luke', the prisoner you've organised to visit in Kerobokan in the morning. The 31-year-old foreigner (whose anonymity you've promised to respect) is waiting to be shot for smuggling 400 grams of heroin in capsules in his stomach. He was originally sentenced to life imprisonment but had his sentence upgraded to death after appealing. You've arranged the meeting through Ed Trotter, the Australian pastor dubbed the spiritual advisor to the Bali Nine.

Life in Kerobokan can be harsh, with media reports putting the ration at a banana, some pawpaw, five slices of white bread and half a bowl of vegetables a day. The jail doesn't provide coffee or tea, toiletries, clothes, medicine or work. Showers consist of a bucket of water. Metal bunks or floor space are provided, but not mattresses or bedding. Those who can afford the 'room rent' can upgrade, but otherwise they're stuck in what's known as a *cel tikus* – a rat cell.

By Western standards, Kerobokan seems squalid and corrupt, but it reflects the living standards of so many of those smiling waiters. And with sufficient money and outside connections, a sentence here can actually be preferable to the rigidities of the Australian penal system. Trotter certainly believes some of the Bali Nine may prefer to stay in Kerobokan rather than be repatriated.

Western prisons, Australian prisons, seem to be much more severe. There is that informality and relatively casual nature about the Indonesian prisons, even though the system of justice may be a bit more lax than what we'd expect in Australia. There is also a growing group of carers here and it looks like a supportive connection with the Australian and other foreign prisoners will continue for the long haul.

Prisoners in Kerobokan can receive whatever their visitors bring in and are able to furnish their cells; run mobile phones, fans, TVs and laptops; and buy beer and even drugs. Most of these things are illegal but in Kerobokan money moves mountains. A day trip outside for medical treatment is said to cost about $120. Another prisoner told *The Sydney Morning Herald* he'd paid $35,000 to get his sentence reduced from twelve years to five.

Given that Kerobokan's famous Australians are inundated with family and hungry journalists, you've asked for the name of one of the foreigners who doesn't usually receive visitors bearing life-sustaining supplies. Trotter has SMS-ed a contact inside the jail and this contact has suggested Luke.

You've already packed a bag of supplies but are worried your care package isn't caring enough, that it doesn't contain enough distractions, enough protein, enough salvation. You've been advised to include cash so Luke can purchase intra-prison contraband but this seems so impersonal – like giving a gift voucher at Christmas. Reading material is also recommended and you've included an all-in-one version of the *Narnia* chronicles, a huge brick of a book you hope Luke will view in terms of its escapist potential rather than its youthful target demographic.

One of the few people who has visited Luke is foreign prisoner activist Kay Danes, the Brisbane mother of three who, along with her husband, Kerry, spent ten months in a Laos jail accused of sapphire smuggling in 2000. The couple vehemently denied the allegations and they were released in October 2001 after high-level government negotiations. Kay, the author of *Nightmare in Laos: The True Story of a Woman Imprisoned in a Communist Gulag*, is now an advocate for the Foreign Prisoners Support Service which lobbies on behalf of other inmates rotting away in foreign dungeons. Kay says Kerobokan is actually one of the better Asian jails. While imprisoned in Laos, she lived off watery pig fat soup and a small serving of sticky rice full of husks and stones. 'Sometimes they made us eat the fish paste that the prison guards made from catfish bred in sewage,' she says. 'The fish were contaminated and covered with sores.'

Kay has recommended a Balinese cab driver called Simon who helped her with the daunting logistics of entering Kerobokan and who also shared a quiet cigarette with Luke once they were inside. Simon is a Christian but arrives at your hotel with a bamboo offering tucked under his windscreen wipers because today is the day Hindus place offerings on weapons and metal. Simon says he has no problem fitting in with Hindu customs because most people in Bali have no problem accommodating his Christian ones. They wish him a happy Christmas and he puts the relevant offerings under his wipers.

Simon helps you shop for extra supplies for Luke at the heavily guarded Bintang supermarket in Seminyak. He grabs a plastic basket and quickly collects what's required: toilet paper, soap, anti-dandruff shampoo, Tim Tams, bottled water, and Western and Indonesian cigarettes. You ask if these are Luke's brands and Simon laughs wryly. 'He's in prison,' he says. 'Everything's his brand.'

After the shopping you collect Trotter who has agreed to assist with the paperwork and bribery required for prison access. Trotter is 55 and a pastor with CRC Churches International, a Pentecostal Protestant Christian denomination based in Australia. The first time he visited Bali in 1986 with a parish church he experienced terrible culture shock – not when he arrived but when he returned home to wintry Melbourne. 'When I came to Bali that first time, I felt like I was coming home,' he says. 'It was a life-changing experience. After that first visit, I felt life was just blown apart. I became very restless back in Australia.'

Trotter – a tall, pleasant-looking fellow who dresses casually and is a keen mobile phone texter – now lives in Legian where he rents a bedsit from a typical Hindu extended family in a typical Hindu compound:

Compared with Aussie urban neighbourhoods, it's bustling, noisy and congested with people, motor-bikes, dogs, cats, lots of animated conversations and laughter. The family is hospitable, full of greetings and smiles – that is, typically Balinese. We chat over cups of coffee. They expect everyone to share their food on special feast days which is no problem, it's delicious.

Trotter enjoys waking up feeling like he's in the middle of a *National Geographic* documentary but says his work in the prison can be draining. Asked what keeps him going, he says the cliché of biblical faith – that and pirate *Seinfeld* DVDs.

With his astounding humanity, humour and dislike of aggressive evangelism, Trotter is a far cry from the intoler-ant missionary stereotype. He points out, for instance, a reference in Hebrews 13:3, where empathy is urged regarding prisoners:

This is in stark contrast to comments made by Prime Minister Howard after the Bali Nine had received their final sentences. He expressed sympathy to their families and friends, but basically said there was no way he could be sympathetic towards the Nine. Yet this text is calling for an extraordinary empathy.

Then there are Trotter's strong views on Indonesia's notoriously harsh drug laws:

> If drug-trafficking continues from and within South-East Asia under the patronage or sponsorship of powerful people – including politicians, military figures and business people – then severe sentences for the 'little fish' are hypocritical. The Bali Nine are just little fish. In Bali such hypocrisy is compounded by an inept and arrogant judicial system. The fact that presiding judges regularly nodded off during hearings at the Denpasar courthouse is outrageous. As is the *pasar narkoba* – the thriving drug market within Kerobokan Prison. Also a walk down Jalan Legian for any tourist may provide the opportunity to purchase anything from mushrooms, ganja, cocaine, heroin and ecstasy. So much for 'Bali's drug-free image' that one judge boasted about before sentencing Schapelle.

Kerobokan Prison is said to have eclipsed Kuta Beach as the prime attraction for Australian tourists but most of the folk milling round its curved white walls and wire-topped fences look local. Trotter helps you sign in which requires writing down Luke's name and offence in a registration book. Outside the prison's main entrance is a crush of visitors clutching giant plastic bags full of instant noodles and toilet rolls. Every so often a guard on the inside opens the door a fraction and everyone pushes violently to get in.

Trotter throws himself into this extreme sport with well-practised gusto, though he says that – inexplicably enough – the entry procedure changes every time he comes. On the other side of the gate is another registration desk which requires the handing over of passports, mobile phones and bribes. You follow Trotter's lead and put the cash down with your passport like it's the most natural thing in the world. You'd expected this to be one of the most stressful parts of prison entry but compared to the front door body slam, it's an absolute breeze.

The two of you walk through to the visiting area, an agreeable white courtyard with gardens, wall murals, a white and ginger prison cat and a guy with a puppy. Like the streets outside, there is also a plethora of relentless peddlers, many of whom are entrepreneurial inmates. A dodgy small-time crim from the nearby island of Lombok opens a bottle of Fanta and plonks it down on the cement in front of you before you have a chance to say you don't want it. 'Drink it yourself,' you tell him. 'Why, thank you,' he replies, skolling it before demanding you pay him double his original asking price. 'But you offered to buy it for me!' he insists, scandalised. You pay the crook for the Fanta and then give him another 5000 rupiah (A70c) to rent two dirty cane mats to sit on, and another 5000 rupiah to go into the jail to find Luke. Trotter says this is one of the big problems with the Kerobokan visiting 'system'. Just because you make it as far as the visiting yard doesn't mean anyone will tell your prisoner you're here. He says the relatives of detained Australians who don't know the rules sometimes sit for hours waiting in vain.

Matthew Norman, one of the youngest members of the Bali Nine, arrives looking tall, slouchy and extraordinarily ordinary. The twenty-year-old's hair has only just started growing back after he shaved it for his sentencing two weeks earlier, a measure he joked was to ensure he didn't have a hair out of place in court. You try not to eavesdrop on his conversation with Trotter while you wait for Luke but it's hard not to. Norman is pissed off at all the errors in the Australian Bali Nine media coverage. One reporter wrote that Norman watched a *Police Academy* DVD while waiting for his life sentence. 'But that's just shit,' he says. 'I hate that shit.' He adds that his mum recently brought him two hundred pirate DVDs but that he has sent most of them back.

The pastor and the prisoner seem relaxed and fond of each other. Trotter doesn't mention God and Norman doesn't curtail his smoking or swearing. The swift Christian conversions of members of the Bali Nine have copped a lot of flak in the media but Trotter says he has great confidence in the spiritual commitment of his two closest Bali Nine friends, Norman and Andrew Chan. If they can avoid the firing squad, it really is possible to imagine these young Australians finding some solace in their new religions, routines and relationships. Bali Nine mule Renae Lawrence, for instance, is said to have developed a strong friendship with Schapelle Corby and even has a new lover, a Balinese woman who shares her cell.

Luke finally arrives and you introduce yourself awkwardly, feeling like you're on a weird blind date. The conversation is stilted and you both stare off into space searching for something to say. Luke's a man of few words and – not surprisingly – is obsessed with his sentence. When he does talk, it's usually about other prisoners who got less time for greater drug crimes. Asked what's been happening in the prison lately, he says the electricity has been down for four days because one of the Westerners is running a minibar fridge and it keeps shorting the prison circuitry. Like Norman and the other Australians, Luke's status as a foreign prisoner (there are only thirty out of a total of about 759) means he stands out here both culturally and physically.

As you chat, you can't help thinking about what will happen if Luke's subsequent appeals are unsuccessful. Under Indonesian execution procedures, condemned criminals are taken to a secret location, usually in the middle of the night, where a red target is marked on their chests and they are blindfolded and tied to a pole or tree. A non-voluntary firing squad of either twelve or fourteen elite policemen then choose from a line of rifles lying on the ground – only two of which have live rounds. The executioners are told to aim for the heart, but death does not always come quickly. A man who helped with a 1995 execution told *The Sydney Morning Herald* that his victim kept gasping for breath for nearly five minutes. 'It was like being part of a murder,' he said. 'Everyone was quiet and everyone could hear him wheezing, fighting for breath. You know, the heart was broken but the body kept breathing.'

It's a barbaric price to have to pay for what was – in Luke's case – a mere 31 capsules of heroin.

Before you leave, you realise you've forgotten to put any cash in Luke's care package. You reach into your wallet, screw up what you hope is a suitably hefty wad and try to subtly shove it into one of the Bintang shopping bags. Later you realise you accidentally cleaned yourself out completely.

After the jail, you sit shell-shocked with Simon at an Indian chain restaurant. Too distressed to discuss Luke, you talk instead about the bribery required for prison entry. Simon bemoans the corruption. 'But those guards have families, too,' you say. 'No mercy for the corrupt,' is the cabbie's curt reply. He's far more forgiving of raucous holidaymakers. Asked what he thinks of wild Australian behaviour in Bali, Simon says it's fine. 'After all, they're on holidays,' he says. 'What's it matter if they're yelling in the streets so long as they don't make any crimes?'

One of the last things you do before you fly home is visit Jimbaran Bay, the site of the second bombing. As you walk along the beach, desperate maître d's sprint from their abandoned cafés trying to drag you up to their empty tables. 'Not even just for coffee?' cries one. 'Not even just for juice?' Row after row of beachside seafood restaurants stand empty, the glass tanks built for live seafood drained and dry. It's the lunchtime peak hour and there are only two other white people on the beach – a pair of large Germans who struggle to manoeuvre their plastic seats in the sand. Under the tables feral dogs sleep, fight and fuck. Down by the sand is a bamboo offering containing a cigarette and an ageing potato. The demons here have base tastes.

You leave that night after battling through a security fest that makes Ku De Ta look laissez faire. At Ngurah Rai airport, there is a grand total of twelve document and security checks before you're allowed to board the plane. First an x-ray and metal-detector check required for entry to the terminal. Then a pre-check-in check-in where armed guards open your mega case and sift through the contents with an explosive detection device. Then check-in, pre-customs check-in, customs check-in and post customs check-in, followed by yet another set of x-raying and metal detection. After that there's a further documents check. Then just one more batch of x-rays and metal detection.

The pièce de résistance is a full-body pat-down which involves bawdy inner thigh, groin and breast circling that'd have the pornography bill's anti-sensualist spies apoplectic. This is followed by an aggressive bag search during which a seething guard attacks your toiletry bag and opens every item of make-up, screaming at you to stand back as he twists out a pale pink lipstick. Another passenger runs into strife with a portable umbrella. The angry guard is so outraged by its pop-out button, he looks as if he's ready to open fire.

As you return your terrorist toiletries to their rightful pouches, you wonder whether all this lipstick and umbrella paranoia will really stop the next extremist hell-bent on blowing up infidels or whether, like so many other overt anti-terrorism measures, it merely serves to distract Western travellers from their inevasible vulnerability.

The umbrella's owner, meanwhile, is still making a guilty-sounding and wildly inadequate attempt to explain herself. In her nervousness and fear, the quotidian has suddenly become completely inexplicable.

EIGHT

What Bombs?

As you wait in the final airport lounge for the final boarding pass check, you ask other passengers about their holidays and why they ignored the travel warnings. Three couples in a row blame the beautiful Balinese. Two bolshy English backpackers (no doubt wearing *Fuck Terrorists – They're Bollocks* T-shirts beneath their fashionably tattered denims) say they came because staying away is just what those bastard bombers want, innit.

Everyone else says, 'What travel warnings?'

Their ignorance is mind-blowing. In fact, they strike you as exactly the sort of folk who made the most noise during the Corby trial – those tunnel-visioned objectors who actually thought Indonesia would listen to their myopic rantings and think: 'Hmm. Australians are threatening to kill our diplomats, retract their tsunami donations and call us more chimp names on the radio. The best way to save face is to acquiesce and set Schapelle free at once.'

As corporate globalisation shrinks the planet, wealthy

89

Westerners seem increasingly complacent about foreign travel in the third world. Everyone's happy to book a cheap holiday in sunny downtown Sri Lanka, oh-so-authentic Vietnam or you beauty Bali, but no one wants to accept they might also have to negotiate alien (and comparatively inadequate) hospitals, bureaucracies and judiciaries; to accept that there's a reason the shopping and the service is so cheap. Learning about and respecting the third-world status quo should be Travel Survival 101 for holidaymakers in South-East Asia. But governments are a different matter. Governments should rage against the machine, should do whatever is within their power to insist on transparent and independent judicial process, humane prison conditions and the abolition of the death penalty.

'Not that human rights are ever likely to trump diplomacy when it comes to Canberra's dealings with Jakarta,' you tell the greasy accountant sitting next to you on the plane after he insists on making conversation. 'We have too much to gain from keeping things cosy to kick up a stink. Two-way trade in 2004 was almost $A8.5 billion and Indonesia is the largest source of Australia's lucrative foreign student supply. SBY was also Australia's most dedicated backer when we were lobbying for an invitation to the inaugural East Asia Summit last year. It must drive those Canberra pollies nuts knowing all those pesky Indonesian Muslims are Australia's pass card to the sweet markets of East Asia.'

The greasy accountant – who hauls off his sweater to reveal a *Jiggy Jig* T-shirt – is unimpressed, even when you tell him former prime minister Paul Keating once estimated that a strategically benign Indonesia saved Australia $35 billion a year on security costs alone. 'Did you make it to the Cabana Club at the Hard Rock Café in Kuta?' the greasy accountant asks. 'Now that was something.'

Your travelling companion puts on his headphones to watch *Walk the Line* on a fly-swot of a screen miles up the aisle and for the rest of the trip the two of you fight for elbow room on the bony armrest. Most of the time the war is discreet. You inadvertently remove your elbow to open your hermetically sealed sachet of nuts and he takes the opportunity to wedge his arm in. He dozes off during the movie and you take the opportunity to accrue as much new real estate as possible. After a while, however, the two of you stop Mr Nice Guying and just start pushing.

All this makes you think of Australia and Indonesia and their relatively tiny slice of shared sea, even more. They're just like us, you want to tell the greasy accountant. A couple of punters with nothing in common who have no choice but to try and get along because they've been forced to sit next to each other on a long, long trip. And Bali? Why Bali's just like the armrest …

The metaphor is so laboured you decide one plastic beaker of putrid plane wine is definitely your limit.

As the jet jolts through the night you wonder how long it will be before the age of terror turns into the age of something else and Australians return to their backyard Balinese playground in their old numbers. Despite the gloomy predictions, you know eventually they will. Bali's just too close, too easy, too Bing-Crosby-Bob-Hope exotic to ignore. And like any other long-term relationship, breaking up is hard to do.

You've certainly never been able to call it quits. Time and again you travel to Bali and time and again you're turned off by the tourist canker and swear the fling is finished. Then, within weeks of returning home, you forget the crowds and all-night diarrhoea and start missing the place: yearning for the spicy duck and pork, the for-God's-sake-get-a-camera beauty of the terraced rice paddies and the fragrant aroma of clove cigarettes that permeates everything.

Memory experts say this is a common phenomenon. Humans have idealised expectations that reality can never match, but our rose-coloured anticipation is matched by equally rose-coloured retrospection. It doesn't matter how much we hate the tacky carvings, the relentless hucksters and the food poisoning while we're there. If what we expect from Bali is suckling piglet, scrumptious jungle and smoky cloves, that's what we'll remember. What actually happens is almost irrelevant.

Given all this (and given the extraordinary insularity of the 'What travel warnings?' comments), it doesn't seem so inconceivable that one day the sunburned couples queuing at Ngurah Rai will be asking 'What drug cases?', 'What executions?', 'What bombs?'. And maybe this isn't such a bad thing. Short memory syndrome and selective recollection don't get a great wrap from historians and psychologists, but holidays, foreign policies and new love affairs wouldn't have a hope in hell without them.

When you get home, the city looks unbearably neat and anal, the same way it always does after the chaos of Bali. When you get home, you unbolt your mega case and a cloud of Seminyak mosquitoes flies out a side pocket. When you get home, your phone rings and it's Luke, calling from a friend's blackmarket mobile. He's worried you accidentally left a stack of money in his shopping bag and wants to know if he can return it somehow. It takes an age to collect yourself and tell him to forget it, it's his.

As you unpack your new *Suicide Glam* T-shirt, you

remember that Luke was arrested while travelling on a forged passport with a fake name and nationality which means his family and real government don't even know he's in prison which means that if his execution goes ahead, he won't even die as himself. For the umpteenth time, you're struck by all this death, all this despair, all this diabolism so close to home.

Short memory syndrome and selective recollection definitely have their advantages but it doesn't take much to realise that, beneath the booze and bikinis, Bali is very different from all those platitudes pumped out about paradise.

Holiday island also has its horrors.

Notes on Sources

The following sources were consulted when writing this book.

Books

Jeremy Allan, *Bali Blues*, Media Makara, Denpasar, 2005.

Italo Calvino, *Mr Palomar*, Picador, London, 1986.

Italo Calvino, *If On a Winter's Night a Traveller*, Vintage, London, 1998.

Eric Oey ed., *Periplus Guide to Bali: The Island of the Gods*, Periplus Editions, Singapore, 2005.

Ryan Ver Berkmoes, Lisa Steer Guérard and Jocelyn Harewood, *Bali and Lombok*, 10th edition, Lonely Planet, Melbourne, 2005.

Adrian Vickers, *Bali: A Paradise Created*, Penguin Books, Melbourne, 1989.

Richard White, *A History of Getting Away in Australia*, Pluto Press Australia, Melbourne, 2005.

Cindy Wockner and Madonna King, *One-way Ticket*, HarperCollins, Sydney, 2006.

Newspapers and Magazines

A. Amirrachman, 'Australia–RI ties tested', *Jakarta Post*, 1 June 2005, p. 6.

G. Ansley, 'Neighbourhood watch', *New Zealand Herald*, 9 April 2005, p. B13.

S. Astbury, 'Huge gulf yawns over the neighbourhood fence', *Bangkok Post* (reprinted in *Daily Telegraph*, 24 August 2005, p. 31).

'Bali bombing site a car park', *Daily Telegraph*, Edition 4: City Edition, 28 December 2005, p. 18.

'Bali slips decency reforms', *Australian*, Edition 1, 7 March 2006, p. 10.

C. Banham, 'Bilateral bond a thin veneer over suspicion', *Sydney Morning Herald*, 25 July 2005, p. 9.

G. Barker, 'Dangers of trial outcry', *Australian Financial Review*, 30 May 2005, p. 62.

R. Bonner, 'Indonesia drug case brings out the worst', *International Herald Tribune*, 10 June 2005, p. 3.

A. Burrell, 'Enrolments from Indonesia boom', *Australian Financial Review*, 8 December 2003, p. 31.

'Consolidating regional ties', *Australian Financial Review*, 6 April 2005, p. 62.

M. Cook, 'Reaching out to Indonesia', *Herald-Sun*, 11 January 2005, p. 17.

I. Cotan, 'I–Australia ties: East Timor, Bali bombing, tsunami and beyond', *Jakarta Post*, 5 March 2005, p. 7.

S. Creedy, 'Garuda axes flights as tourists give Bali a miss', *Australian*, 1 June 2006, p. 8.

J. Dickins, 'Aussies shun Indonesian trips', *Sunday Telegraph*, 9 April 2006, p. 31.

A. Dupont, 'Neighbours back on track', *Australian Financial Review*, 31 March 2005, p. 63.

D. Durber, 'Racism within Australian culture', *Jakarta Post*, 4 June 2005, p. 7.

E. Ellis, 'Carousels of suspicion – the Corby effect', *Bulletin*, 7 June 2005, vol. 123, no. 23.

F. Farouque and L. Gooch, 'The Bali backlash', *Age*, 31 May 2005, p.15.

G. Fealy, 'Between the rhetoric and the reality of SBY', *Canberra Times*, 4 April 2005, p. 13.

R. Fitzgerald, 'Morality bill will threaten diversity', *Australian*, Edition 1, 24 April 2006, p. 8.

M. Forbes and K. Rompies, 'Navel gazing ruled out as Indonesians button up', *Sydney Morning Herald*, 25 February 2006, p. 17.

M. Forbes and K. Rompies, 'Islamic moral drive spreads fear in Indonesia – woman jailed for lipstick in bag', *Sydney Morning Herald*, 11 March 2006, p. 21.

M. Forbes, 'Abandoned Bali waits in hope', *Sydney Morning Herald*, 1 May 2006, p. 12.

M. Gebicki, 'Back to Bali – the island's best deals – return to paradise', *Sun-Herald*, 26 October 2003, p. T1.

M. Gordon, 'New era for Australia–Indonesia relations', *Sunday Age*, 21 November 2004, p. 7.

P. Hartcher, 'Howard's neighbourhood watch', *Sydney Morning Herald*, 3 June 2005, p. 13.

P. Jennings, 'Australia's regional diplomacy challenge', *Australian Financial Review*, 30 April 2005, p. 63.

P. Kelly, 'A fair trial, but not in our media', *Australian*, 1 June 2005, p. 15.

P. Kelly, 'The day foreign policy won Asia', *Australian*, 6–7 August 2005, p. 17.

M. Lane, 'The hypocrisy of an imperialist down under', *Jakarta Post*, 4 June 2005, p. 7.

T. Lindsey and P. Gillespie, 'Case of a weak defence', *Sydney Morning Herald*, 19 April 2005, p. 13.

M. Moore and K. Rompies, 'Executioner's trigger itches, but Amrozi may grow old', *Sydney Morning Herald*, 4 August 2003, p. 1.

M. Moore, 'Echoes of Corby case in French prisoner's tale', *Sydney Morning Herald*, 16 April 2005, p. 17.

M. Moore, 'On the inside life's not that bad, if you have money', *Sydney Morning Herald*, 28 May 2005, p. 6.

I. Munro, G. Tippet, L. Murdoch, C. Munro and A. Smith, 'An island apart – Bali's agony', *Sydney Morning Herald*, 8 October 2005, p. 25.

R. Neill, 'For most women, intimacy is never skin deep', *Australian*, 2 February 2002, p. 11.

T. Nguyen, 'The ugly ocker rears his racist head once more', *Australian*, 20 July 2005, p. 15.

S. O'Malley, 'Indo–Aussie relations', *Geelong Advertiser*, 5 April 2005, p. 6.

L. Oakes, 'Unlocking Schapelle', *Bulletin*, 31 May 2005, vol. 123, no. 22.

S. Powell, 'Howard goes courting', *Australian*, 20 October 2004, p. 13.

S. Powell, 'Raids take the ecstasy out of Kuta raves', *Australian*, 27–28 August 2005, p. 19.

S. Powell, 'Smugglers' "leader" may be island's first execution', *Australian*, 26 January 2006, p. 5.

R. Sackville, 'Don't hold the Bali court in contempt', *Australian*, 1 June 2005, p. 15.

D. Shanahan, 'Australian anger will condemn those in Bali', *Australian*, 29 April 2005, p. 13.

I. Susanti, 'Corby's sentence won't affect RI–Australia ties', *Jakarta Post*, 1 June 2005, p. 12.

E. Tom, 'Bananas over Bali', *Sydney Morning Herald*, Travel section, 19 May 1994, p. 26.

P. Toohey, 'The curse of the Corby clan', *Bulletin*, 31 January 2006, pp. 15–19.

T. Watkins, M. Kay and NZPA, 'Howard tries to cool fury on Corby', *Dominion Post*, 3 June 2005, p. 1.

P. Weston and C. Wockner, 'Corby jail a tourist attraction', *Sunday Telegraph*, 19 March 2006, p. 25.

W. Witoelar, 'Changing perceptions of Australia post-Corby trial', *Jakarta Post*, 9 July 2005, p. 7.

C. Wockner, 'How Amrozi will die – former executioner tells of firing squad', *Sunday Telegraph*, Edition 6, 10 August 2003, p. 7.

C. Wockner, 'Bali bombers prepared to face the death squad', *Sunday Telegraph*, Edition 1, 21 August 2005, p. 75.

S.B. Yudhoyono, 'A comprehensive partnership', *Australian*, 5 April 2005, p. 13.

Online Resources

'Aussies flock to Bali despite drugs cases', *Age*, 5 May 2005. Available: http://www.theage.com.au/news/World/Aussies-flock-to-Bali-despite-drugs-cases/2005/05/05/1115092605616.html [16 September 2005].

'Australia–Indonesia relations remain strong: Howard', *Australian Broadcasting Corporation*, 3 June 2005. Available from Factiva: Document ABCNEW0020050603e16300065 [2 September 2005].

'Australia–Indonesia ties to continue strengthening: Yudhoyono', *Asia Pulse*, 5 April 2005. Available from Factiva: Document AAPFIN0020050405e145000ru [2 September 2005].

'Australian aid package a watershed for Canberra–Jakarta relations: analysts', *Agence France-Presse*, 6 January 2005. Available from Factiva: Document AFPR000020050106e116002mh [2 September 2005].

S. Baden and S. O'Malley, 'Indon Aust relationship to strengthen as business opps grow', *Australian Associated Press*, 5 April 2005. Available from Factiva: Document DJI0000020050602e1620005g [2 September 2005].

'Bali bikinis to stay', *Age*, 6 March 2006. Available: http://www.theage.com.au/articles/2006/03/06/114149 3604475.html?from=top5 [29 June 2006].

'Bali or bust', *Standard Weekend*, 27 May 2006, Available: http://www.thestandard.com.hk/weekend_news_detai l.asp?pp_cat=30&art_id=19506&sid=8030509&con_ type=3&d_str=20060527 [30 June 2006].

V. Brooks, 'Embassy incident to test mettle of Australia–Indon ties', *Dow Jones Newswires*, 2 June 2005. Available from Factiva: Document AAPFIN0020050405e145000ru [2 September 2005].

'Busted – Australia and Indonesia', *Economist*, 4 June 2005. Available from Factiva: Document EC00000020050603e16400005 [2 September 2005].

I. Cotan, 'Indonesia–Australian relations: East Timor, Bali bombing, tsunami and beyond', *Australian Embassy of the Republic of Indonesia*, 1 March 2005. Available: http://www.kbri-canberra.org.au/speeches/2005/ 050301e.htm [2 September 2005].

R. Cribb, 'The dark side of giving: Australia–Indonesia relations post-tsunami', *Asian Studies Association of Australia*, January 2005. Available: http://coombs. anu.edu.au/SpecialProj/ASAA/asian-currents-archive/ asian-currents-05-01.html [2 September 2005].

A. Downer, T. Lindsey and C. Adams, 'Australia–Indonesia Relations – new directions', *Asialink*, 25 June 1999. Available: http://www.asialink.unimelb.edu.au/cpp/transcripts/downer.html [2 September 2005].

D. Flitton, 'Foreign policy: guided by the masses or the elite?', *Online Opinion*, 17 June 2005. Available: http://www.onlineopinion.com.au/view.asp?article= 3565 [14 September 2005].

Foreign Prisoners Support Service. Available: www.foreign-prisoners.com [29 June 2006].

J. Gershman, 'Is Southeast Asia the second front?' *Foreign Affairs*, October 2002, Available: http://www.foreign affairs.org/20021001faupdate10329/john-gershman/is-southeast-asia-the-second-front.html [15 September 2005].

B. Guerin, 'Drugs: high noon in Indonesia', *Asia Times*, 3 September 2005. Available: http://www.atimes.com/atimes/Southeast_Asia/GI03Ae01.html [3 September 2005].

Z.P. Hakim, 'Business as usual despite bombings, politics, Corby', *Jakarta Post*, 16 September 2005, Available: http://www.thejakartapost.com/community/aus3.asp [16 September 2005].

'Indonesia's dilemma', *Standard Weekend*, 6 May 2006, Available: http://www.thestandard.com.hk/weekend_news_detail.asp?pp_cat=31&art_id=18092&sid=7807 661&con_type=3&d_str=20060506 [30 June 2006].

'Jakarta protest demands death sentence for Corby', *Age*, 4 June 2005. Available: http://www.theage.com.au/news/World/Jakarta-protest-demands-death-sentence-for-Corby/2005/06/04/1117825099278.html [14 September 2005].

'Jakarta rage over visas', *Age*, 24 March 2006. Available:

http://www.theage.com.au/news/national/jakarta-rage-over-visas/2006/03/23/1143083906919.html [30 June 2006].

T. Jones and E. Trotter, 'Pastor discusses relationship with Bali nine', *Australian Broadcasting Corporation*, 15 February 2006. Available: http://www.abc.net.au/lateline/content/2006/s1570963.htm [29 June 2006].

P. Kelly, 'Howard eyes new era in Australia–Indonesia relations', *Australian Broadcasting Corporation*, 21 November 2004. Available from Factiva: ABCTRS0020041121e0bl0002 [2 September 2005].

'Miniskirts clash with Islam as Indonesia drafts pornography law', *Bloomberg*, 10 May 2006. Available: http://www.bloomberg.com/apps/news?pid=10000080&sid=at7mE_oU2Jil&refer=asia [29 June 2006].

'Muslim playboy', *Wall Street Journal*, 21 April 2006. Available: http://online.wsj.com/google_login.html?url=http%3A%2F%2Fonline.wsj.com%2Farticle%2FSB114557981761731959.html%3Fmod%3Dgoogle-news_wsj [29 June 2006].

S. O' Malley, 'Will Corby be the splinter in Aust–Indon relationship?', *Australian Associated Press*, 3 June 2005b. Available from Factiva: Document AAP0000020050603e163000um [2 September 2005].

R. Peake, 'When once hostile neighbours begin to get pally', *Khaleej Times*, 3 April 2005. Available: http://www.khaleejtimes.com/ColumnistHome.asp?xfile=data/rosspeake/2005/April/columnistrosspeake_April1.xml&section=rosspeake [2 September 2005].

T. Regan, 'Australia, Indonesia hit rough patch', *Christian Science Monitor*, 17 August 2005. Available: http://www.christiansciencemonitor.com/2005/0819/dailyUpdate.html [2 September 2005].

L. Rieffel, 'Indonesia's quiet revolution', *Foreign Affairs*, September/October 2004. Available: http://www.foreignaffairs.org/20040901faessay83509/lex-rieffel/indonesia-s-quiet-revolution.html [15 September 2005].

S. Senise, 'From Balibo to Tugun: the Corby case in perspective', *The Brisbane Institute*, 2 June 2005. Available: http://www.brisinst.org.au/resources/senise_stephen_balibo_tugun.html [16 September 2005].

T. Sissener, 'The Republic of Indonesia: general and presidential elections April–September 2004', *The Norwegian Centre for Human Rights Report 12/2004*. Available: http://72.14.203.104/search?q=cache:x6vDQew_V88J:www.humanrights.uio.no/forskning/publ/nr/2004/12.pdf+%22popular+in+bali%22+megawati+sukarnoputri&hl=en&ct=clnk&cd=2&lr=lang_en&client=safari [29 June 2006].

Smart Traveller – The Australian Government's Travel Advisory and Consular Assistance Service. Available: http://www.smarttraveller.gov.au/ [29 June 2006].

G. Thompson, 'Howard should convert to Islam: Bashir', *Australian Broadcasting Corporation*, 15 June 2006. Available: http://www.abc.net.au/news/newsitems/200606/s1663330.htm [30 June 2006].

'Too sexy for my Bali!', *Bali Discovery Tours*, 3 December 2005, Available: http://www.balidiscovery.com/messages/message.asp?Id=3060 [29 June 2006].

P. Toohey, 'Bali bombshell', *Bulletin*, 1 July 2005. Available: http://bulletin.ninemsn.com.au/bulletin/site/articleIDs/1888F01D142C6269CA2570100079DC09 [29 June 2005].

Acknowledgements

Special thanks to Justin Tabone, Deborah Shaw, Marie-Pierre Cleret, Ali Titus, Ed Trotter, Helen Corben, Daniel Tom, Russell Eldridge, David McCormack, Paul Toohey, Donni One, Kay Dane, Tony Moore, Fiona Inglis, Pippa Masson, Sarah Crisp and Nadine Davidoff.

For more information on the Foreign Prisoners Support Service see www.foreignprisoners.com.

NOW AUSTRALIA

A refreshing series from Pluto Press featuring new journalism on contemporary issues by Australia's leading writers and journalists.

* *Now Australia* is unashamedly about how we live now, in early 21st Century Australia.

* Stylistically *Now* aims high: to revive the art of the 'reportage' style of writing in Australia, where authors insert themselves into the story, become eye witnesses to the events around them, and participants in the great issues of the day.

* *Now* asks Australia's best writers to look inside the events, institutions and issues of today, challenges orthodoxies, and asks: what, and who, do we want to be in the 21st Century?

* *Now* is published five times a year. Each issue of *Now,* features a thought-provoking essay of 20,000 - 25,000 words, broken into chapters, by a high profile author or journalist who has immersed themselves in the day to day life of their subject.

* In the spirit of the reportage genre, our authors are story tellers occupying the space where literature meets journalism meets politics.

* With writers of imagination, skill, experience and profile, *Now* will always entertain and provoke readers with new ideas.

We want to hear from NOW readers. If you have any thoughts on issues that could be explored by NOW Australia please submit to now@nowaustralia.com.au.

Visit www.nowaustralia.com.au to share your thoughts about NOW Australia and see what others are saying.

PLUTO PRESS AUSTRALIA

The first book in the new series **NOW Australia** – new journalism on contemporary issues by Australia's leading writers and journalists.

Inside the Lifestyles of the Rich & Tasteful
By Andrew West

With wry humour and cutting irony, Andrew West observes the customs, privileges, spending and preoccupations of Australia's well-to-do.

West's *grand tour* uncovers the secrets of open days at leading private schools, exclusive sea and tree change retreats, sophisticated dinner parties, fashionable shopping districts, exotic holidays and high status jobs.

Here he finds an upper middle class riven by those seduced by money and those obsessed with cultural attainment. He writes of a new class conflict that secretly fashions Australian politics – the materialists versus the culturists.

From Hunters Hill to Byron Bay, Carlton to Balmain, Toorak to Paddington, the culturists and the materialists are fighting the lifestyle wars. Their conflict spills over into politics, and the long simmering culture wars. Much more than a clash of politics, it is a clash of taste and consumption.

After ten years of John Howard's government, the materialists seem to be politically ascendant, while the culturists must console themselves with their private good taste.

But the two groups do have something in common: they can both be real snobs.

ISBN: 186403 337 1 | RRP $17.95 | September 2006

www.nowaustralia.com

PLUTO PRESS AUSTRALIA

Women of the Gobi
Journeys on The Silk Road

Kate James

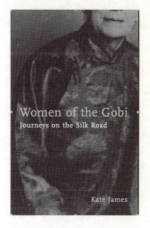

Armed with a copy of *Monkey* and a Mandarin phrasebook, young Australian writer Kate James travelled across the deserts of northwest China in the footsteps of three early 20th century missionaries and their adopted daughter.

Kate became drawn to the writings of this trio of extraordinary women, Mildred Cable and the sisters Eva and Francesca French, who spent most of their lives in China, adopted a deaf Mongolian girl called Topsy and braved sandstorms and warlords to cross the barren Gobi desert on a Bible-laden donkey cart five times between 1923 and 1936.

Tired of aimless travel and the backpacker scene, Kate James decided to follow the 'trio' through the sands, from their girls school in central China along the Silk Road into Central Asia, the monasteries of Tibet and China's Muslim provinces.

Along the way she met a young Living Buddha who liked to draw cars, ate yak hot-pot, was groped by a monk, went briefly mad with altitude sickness, breathed in too much second-hand cigarette smoke and watched China knocking down its historic neighbourhoods and brushing up on its English skills in preparation for the 2008 Olympic Games.

Throughout the journey, the lapsed evangelical was surprised at how much she drew inspiration from the three women missionaries of last century. She also discovered something amazing in following their footsteps: after nearly sixty years of communism, religion was now thriving in China. Like socialism, it had taken on Chinese characteristics.

This is a beautifully written travel tale - full of humour and adventure - about a part of the world shrouded in mystery.

ISBN: 1 86403 353 3 │RRP $29.95│ October 2006

For details on all Pluto Press Australia books visit our website:
www.plutoaustralia.com

PLUTO PRESS AUSTRALIA

A Room in Bombay & Other Stories
Dorothy Wentworth-Walsh

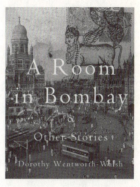

This intriguing and colourful collection of stories was written when the author first visited India in 1949 and during her return in the1980s.

In this beautifully crafted book Dorothy captures an India that is no longer – an India at the time of independence but still marked by colonialism and class, in startlingly fresh style reminiscent of the late Alistair Cooke's *'Letters from America'*.

Contents include: The Queen's Necklace, Caught Short at the Bazaar, Bollywood in the Chawls, That's not Cricket Mr Kipling and The Caftan and the Power of Om.

Her 'reality' journalism is racy but still maintains a sense of dignity and grandeur with a shrewd eye for what is hidden just below the surface.

ISBN: 1 86403 249 9 | RRP $25.95

Last Flight Out of Dili: Memoirs of an Accidental Activist In the Triumph of East Timor
David Scott

The story of the world's newest nation and its incredible struggle to gain independence despite all odds.

This is David Scott's remarkable story of East Timor's rise from 'hopeless cause' to freedom, giving us a unique insight into the people and events that have shaped East Timor's recent turbulent history.

Australian humanitarian aid leader David Scott was in Dili on 28 November, 1975 at the swearing in of the cabinet of the Democratic Republic of East Timor. Next day he was ordered to leave by the Australian Government who were aware of the impending large-scale Indonesian invasion.

Australia's role in these terrible events is critically documented. David Scott uses personal correspondence with José Ramos-Horta to give immediacy to the story. His use of recently released Australian Government documents adds to the intrigue of these dramatic events.

ISBN: 186403 233 2 | RRP $34.95

For details on all Pluto Press Australia books visit our website
www.plutoaustralia.com

PLUTO PRESS AUSTRALIA

On Holidays: A History of Getting Away in Australia   Richard White

White Australia began as a rich man's holiday. Instead of taking the Grand Tour of Europe, Joseph Banks joined Captain Cook's expedition to the South Seas, and transfixed his countrymen with tales of exotic Tahitian women and the natural wonders of Botany Bay – the first Pacific Cruise which led to the colonisation of Australia.

So begins this lively history of the holiday in Australia, spanning leisured cruises to frequent flyer points, bush walking to Bali shop-overs, hill stations to mountain resorts, caravans to back packs, surfing safaris to theme parks.

The traditional Australian holiday has become increasingly difficult to find. Over the last decade our holidays have slipped away, as people work longer hours to spend more and find it harder and harder to juggle jobs, family and hobbies.

We are overwhelmed by holiday choices – from island paradises to heritage parks, from gourmet binges to sex tourism, bushwalking to extreme sports, resorts to shopping to ecotourism– at the very moment we have no time to enjoy them. *On Holidays* is the first detailed account of the long struggle to bring about an Australian institution; and its destruction within a generation.

ISBN: 186403 320 7   RRP $32.95

Pacific Paradises: The Discovery of Tahiti and Hawaii   Trevor Lummis

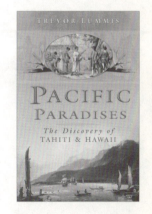

Trevor Lummis tells the powerful and moving story of the discovery of these islands and the lasting impact this had on both Polynesia and Europe.

It is a rich and stirring story of cultures in collison.

Trevor Lummis recreates the lives of the islanders before and after the fateful arrival of the first Europeans and draws upon contemporary letters and diaries to uncover the narrow attitudes of the early explorers. Ironically, western society today embraces many aspects of the islanders' way of life. The noble savages may have been corrupted by so-called civilisation, but their values have survived.

ISBN: 1 86403 297 9   RRP $29.95

For details on all Pluto Press Australia books visit our website:
www.plutoaustralia.com